D1615988

A SIMPLE EXPLANATION OF THE MASS

A SIMPLE EXPLANATION OF THE MASS

A Step-by-Step Commentary on
Each Part of the Mass and
The Seasons of the Liturgical Year

FR. EAMON TOBIN

WELLSPRING
North Palm Beach, Florida

Published by Wellspring

Design by Ashley Wirfel

ISBN: 978-1-63582-105-5 (hardcover)
ISBN: 978-1-63582-117-8 (ebook)

10 9 8 7 6 5 4 3 2 1

Printed in the United States of America

DEDICATION

To Maria Sittig, my wonderful secretary
who has faithfully typed and retyped everything
I have written since 2001.

TABLE OF CONTENTS

INTRODUCTION

"Do this in memory of me." In his book, *The Shape of the Liturgy*, Don Gregory Dix, in reflecting on these words of Jesus, writes:

> *Was ever another command so obeyed? For century after century, spreading slowly to every continent and country and among every race on earth, this action has been done in every conceivable human circumstance for every conceivable human need, from infancy and before it, to extreme old age and after it, from the pinnacles of earthly greatness to the refuge of fugitives in the caves and dens of the earth. Men have found no better thing than this to do for kings at their crowning and for criminals going to the scaffold; for armies in triumph or for a bride and bridegroom in a country church ... for the famine of a whole province or for the soul of a dear lover ... and best of all, week by week, and month by month, on a hundred thousand Sundays, faithfully, unfailingly, across all the parishes of Christendom, priest and people*

continue to work together in order to carry out this command, "Do this in memory of me."

From this beautiful reflection on the Lord's command, one can readily see how important and central the Mass has been to Catholic life down through the ages. In the words: *"Do this in memory of me,"* Jesus commanded the Apostles and their successors to repeat his Eucharistic actions and words, *"until he comes again"* (1 Cor 11:26).

Concerning the centrality of the Eucharist in the life of the Church, the Introduction to the Roman Missal states: *"The celebration of Mass, as the action of Christ and of the People of God arrayed hierarchically, is the center of the whole of Christian life for the Church both universal and local as well as for each of the faithful individually. For in it is found the high point both of the action by which God sanctifies the world in Christ and of the worship that the human race offers to the Father, adoring him through Christ, the Son of God, in the Holy Spirit"* (#16).

Over the centuries, this mystery of our faith has been given a number of names to illumine its saving grace: Breaking of the Bread, Lord's Supper, Holy Sacrifice of the Mass, Eucharistic Assembly, and Liturgy. The word *liturgy* is derived from the Greek *leitourgia* which literally means *work of the people.* When Christians gather together to celebrate *liturgy,* they are participating in the *work of God,* which is our eternal salvation in and through Christ. The *Catechism of the Catholic Church* (herein abbreviated CCC) states: *"Through the Liturgy, our redeemer and high priest continues the work of our redemption in, with and through his Church"* (CCC 1069).

When the bishops of our universal Church gathered in Rome

in the early 1960s for Vatican Council II, they stressed the central importance of the Mass for Catholics. They defined the Mass as the *center of the Christian community, the source and summit of the Christian life,* and *the center and the culmination of the entire life of the Christian community.* Root, source, center, and summit—the Mass is at the heart of our faith and life.

In the *Constitution of the Sacred Liturgy,* the Council Fathers advocated that *"full and active participation by all the people is the aim to be considered before all else: for it is the primary and indispensable source from which the faithful are to derive the true Christian spirit"* (#14).

With regard to the responsibility of pastors in ensuring the full and active participation of the people, the Council Fathers stressed that:

> *Pastors of souls must realize that, when the liturgy is celebrated, more is required than the mere observance of the laws governing valid and licit celebration. It is their duty also to ensure that the faithful take part knowingly, actively and fruitfully. (ibid. #11)*

> *With zeal and patience, pastors of souls must promote the liturgical instruction of the faithful and also their active participation in the liturgy both internally and externally. (ibid. #19)*

> *The Church, therefore, earnestly desires that Christ's faithful, when present at this mystery of faith, should not be there as strangers or silent spectators. On the contrary, through a proper appreciation of the rites and prayers, they should participate knowingly, devoutly, and actively. (ibid. #48)*

As a pastor of many souls in a large parish, it is my hope that this book will help its readers to grow in their understanding and appreciation of the Mass. You will find here a commentary on each part of the Mass and suggestions on how you can enter into the Mass more *consciously, actively* and *fruitfully.* As you will see very shortly, each part of the Mass ends with (a) a *summary* of main points, (b) *questions* for *personal* and *group reflection,* and (c) *good practice* suggestions to develop so that one can enter into the celebration of the Eucharist in a more *active, conscious and fruitful* way.

As you prepare to read the rest of this book on the Mass, it should be inspiring to know the following two realities:

- In modern day Iraq, Catholic families risk their lives to attend Mass on Sundays. In an interview with *60 Minutes,* one young adult said: *"Half of my family goes to one Mass and half to another Mass."* When asked why, the young man answered: *"In this way, if the church is blown up by a terrorist bomb, at least half of my family will survive."*
- In many poor countries, Catholics *walk* one or two hours each way to attend Mass. Such is their dedication to the Eucharist.

In contrast to the above commitment to the Eucharist, millions of Catholics who live in nice homes close to a church and drive nice cars, find it too much of a *sacrifice* or too much of an incon-ven-ience to come to Mass on Sunday. All of us should often pray that the Holy Spirit would open our minds and our hearts to the tremendous gift God is offering us when we choose to actively participate in the Mass.

SUMMARY

- The Mass is a celebration of the death and Resurrection of Jesus Christ.
- Full and active participation in the Mass by all the people is the aim to be considered above all else.

QUESTIONS FOR PERSONAL AND GROUP REFLECTION

- Why has the Mass for 2,000 years been so important for Catholics? How important is it in your life?
- Why do so many Catholics seem to be silent spectators at Mass? Was there a time in your life when you were a silent spectator? If so, what helped to change that?
- When you hear of people making big sacrifices or risking their lives to attend Mass, how does that speak to your heart?

GOOD PRACTICE SUGGESTION

Develop the *good practice* of getting to church ten or more minutes before Mass begins, and remaining at Mass until the end of the final song.

PART ONE: ORDER OF THE MASS

THE MASS
Rooted in Early Christian Traditions

The Mass is not something that mere mortals created. Rather, it is the creation of Jesus himself. This is how St. Paul, writing to Christian converts in Corinth around 60AD, described the institution of the Eucharist.

> *I received from the Lord what I handed on to you, namely, that the Lord Jesus, on the night in which he was betrayed, took bread and after he had given thanks, broke it and said, "This is my body, which is for you. Do this in remembrance of me."*
>
> *In the same way, after the supper, he took the cup, saying, "This cup is the new covenant in my blood. Do this, whenever you drink it, in remembrance of me." Every time, when you eat this bread and drink this cup, you proclaim the death of the Lord until he comes!* (1 Cor 11:23-26)

(For other scriptural references on the institution of the Eucharist, see Mt 26:26-30, Mk 11:22-26, Lk 22:14-20.)

We are very fortunate to have a description of the Mass that was written about 150AD, a little over 100 years after Jesus died. The following description was written by St. Justin Martyr in a letter to a Roman Emperor. The words in brackets are my addition.

On the day we call the day of the sun, all who dwell in the city or country gather in the same place.

The memoirs of the apostles, [reference to writings of the New Testament] *and the writings of the prophets* [Old Testament] *are read, as much as time permits.*

When the reader has finished, he who presides over those gathered admonishes and challenges them to imitate these beautiful things [Homily].

Then we all rise together and offer prayers for ourselves ... and for all others, wherever they may be, so that we may be found righteous by our life and actions, and faithful to the commandments, so as to obtain eternal salvation [General Intercessions].

When the prayers are concluded, we exchange the kiss [Sign of Peace]. *Then someone brings bread and a cup of water and wine mixed together to him who presides over the brethren* [Presentation of Gifts].

He takes them and offers praise and glory to the Father of the universe, through the name of the Son and of the Holy Spirit and for a considerable time he gives thanks that we have been judged worthy of these gifts. When he has concluded the prayers and thanksgiving, all present give voice to an acclamation by saying: "Amen" [Eucharistic Prayer].

When he who presides has given thanks and the people have responded, those whom we call deacons give to those present the "eucharisted" bread, wine and water and take them to those who are absent [Distribution of the Body and Blood of Christ and our pastoral practice of taking communion to the sick and homebound]. (CCC #1345)

It is comforting and important to be aware that the Mass we celebrate today is almost identical in structure and content to the Eucharist that the early Christians celebrated 2,000 years ago. When Catholics gather to celebrate the Eucharist, they are acting in obedience to the Lord's command: *"Do this in memory of me."* Not only that, but they are celebrating this memorial of the Lord's death and Resurrection in a manner very similar to how our ancestors in the faith celebrated the Lord's Supper.

Jesus is present and active at every Mass

Article 27 of the *General Instruction of the Roman Missal* (hereafter abbreviated *GIRM*), a Vatican document which regulates the celebration of the Eucharist, reminds us of the four-fold presence of Christ in the Liturgy.

- Jesus is present in the *assembly* gathered in his name.
- Jesus is present in the *presider* who represents Christ, the head of his Body.

- Jesus is present in the *Word* proclaimed.
- Jesus is present in the *Eucharistic species*—in the bread and wine.

During our celebration of the Lord's Supper, it is Jesus:

- who *calls* us and *gathers* us together so that we might offer fitting worship to God (Intro-ductory Rites).
- who speaks to us when the Word of God is proclaimed (Liturgy of the Word).
- who takes our *prayer of praise and thanks* to the heavenly altar and who shares with us his *Body and Blood* (Liturgy of the Eucharist).
- who *commissions* us to go forth to continue his saving work in the world (Concluding Rites).

The Holy Spirit is also present in our community worship helping us to open our minds and hearts to God and to each other, helping us to worship God in spirit and in truth. Paul reminds us that *"the Spirit helps us in our weakness, for we do not know how to pray as we ought"* (Rom 8:26).

SUMMARY

- The Eucharist is the creation of Jesus.
- The present structure of the Mass has existed since the early days of Christianity.
- Jesus is present in the Eucharist in a four-fold way.

QUESTIONS FOR PERSONAL AND GROUP REFLECTION

- How comforting is it for you to know that our Catholic Mass was instituted by Christ and that the present structure of the Mass is almost identical to how it was celebrated in the early years of Christianity?
- When we talk about the presence of Jesus in the Eucharist, most Catholics only think of his presence in the bread and wine. How might a deeper sense of his presence in the assembly, in the priest, and in the proclaimed Word change the way we enter into the Mass?

GOOD PRACTICE SUGGESTION

Develop the *good practice* of seeing Christ in the people you pray with at Mass, keeping in mind that some of them may be carrying heavy burdens.

RITUAL GESTURES AND POSTURES

Since worship engages Christians fully in every aspect of their being, they worship God with their bodies and feelings as well as their minds and spirits, with their hands and feet as well as their eyes and ears. The non-verbal elements of the Liturgy can express what cannot be articulated in words and, at times, can reinforce the spoken Word. Because of their importance, the gestures and postures of the Liturgy are to be given the attention they require. (Introduction to the Order of the Mass #27)

Our celebration of the Eucharist is filled with many sacred gestures and postures. For example:

- When we enter a church, we *bless ourselves with holy water*—a reminder of our Baptism in Christ.
- Before we enter a pew, we *genuflect* or *bow* as an act of adoration and mark of respect for the Eucharist. Every

Catholic Church has a *Tabernacle* where hosts are kept. Catholics believe that Jesus *continues* to be truly present in the hosts after the celebration of Mass has finished. Each Tabernacle has a lighted sanctuary lamp beside it.

- In Christian liturgical tradition, *standing* is the posture of an Easter people lifted up to greet the Risen Lord. We stand to give praise and thanks to God. We stand when we chant the Gospel acclamation and when we listen to Christ speak to us during the proclamation of the Gospel.
- During Mass, we *sit* to listen and meditate on the Word of God and during the homily.
- We *kneel* before God as an expression of our humble submission to him as our Creator, as a sign of contrition for our sins, and as an act of adoration and reverence.

Other gestures used during Mass include: *bowing* as a natural and gracious sign of respect; *kissing* (the altar and the Book of the Gospels) as a more intense expression of reverence; *joined hands* as an expression of prayerfulness; and *striking the breast* as an act of humility and contrition.

When we carry out external postures and gestures in a dignified way, we honor God and commu-nicate to all around us that we are in a sacred space and involved in a sacred and holy action. The December 2004 edition of the magazine *U.S. Catholic* had an article on the Eucharist, which tells of the beautiful story of a Protestant Minister who attended a Catholic funeral Mass. The author of the article writes:

I learned from a Protestant pastor that if we celebrate Mass with faith and attention and sing with enthusiasm, we are enriching the sacramental experience of everyone else around us.

This local Protestant pastor came to a funeral at our church because the deceased woman had been married to a man from his congregation. Our pastor invited him to proclaim one of the scripture readings, so he was seated near the altar for the whole funeral. On the way down the aisle afterward, our priest noticed tears streaming down the man's face. When they got to the sacristy, the priest asked if he was all right. "Oh, I'm fine," he said. "It's just that the ritual was so sincere." This man came from a church that didn't believe in ritual. They thought that ceremony and ritual were just window dressing, some decorative flourishes that had no meaning. And this man was experiencing for the first time, up close and personal, the power of religious ritual. "The ritual was so sincere" that it moved him to tears. It was so powerful that he started coming to weekday Mass at our church and attended a whole year of RCIA sessions (Rite of Christian Initiation of Adults).

Interestingly, only once did this man experience the sincerity of our rituals from standing by the altar next to our pastor. All the other times he experienced it in the pews from the way parishioners participated and prayed. It made me realize more deeply that we all help to make our liturgical rituals sincere. The question raised by the incident is: If a visitor or neighbor or children from our own family watch us participate at Mass, will they comment on how sincere the ritual is? Will they be moved to tears?

SUMMARY

- At Mass, we worship God not only with our spirit but with our whole being.
- When ritual is carried out prayerfully and with reverence, it has the power to touch us deeply and to touch those around us.

QUESTIONS FOR PERSONAL AND GROUP REFLECTION

- Can you recall a time when a liturgical ritual touched you in a very powerful way? If so, what do you think made that ritual so powerful?
- The big danger with liturgical rituals is that we carry them out in a rote and mindless way. What can help us to avoid this pitfall? What helps you to carry out liturgical rituals and postures in a prayerful way?

GOOD PRACTICE SUGGESTION

Develop the *good practice* of performing ritual actions in a prayerful and reverent way, e.g., making the sign of the cross slowly and reverently, bowing and genuflecting with reverence, exchanging the sign of peace with a sense of the presence of Christ in those around us.

THE FOUR PARTS OF THE MASS:

I. **Introducy Rites**
II. **Liturgy of the Word**
III. **Liturgy of the Eucharist**
IV. **Concluding Rites**

The two main parts of the Mass are the Liturgy of the Word and the Liturgy of the Eucharist. But as GIRM reminds us, these two parts are *"so closely interconnected that they form but* ***one single act of worship****. For in the Mass, the table both of God's Word and of Christ's Body is prepared from which the faithful may be instructed and refreshed"* (#28).

I. INTRODUCTORY RITES

The purpose of the Introductory Rites *"is to ensure that the faithful who come together as one establish communion and dispose themselves to listen properly to God's Word and to celebrate the Eucharist worthily"* (GIRM #46).

The Introductory Rites of the Mass consist of:

- Entrance Procession and Song
- Sign of the Cross and Greeting
- Penitential Act
- Gloria
- Collect

Entrance Procession and Song

The Mass begins when the Cantor invites the assembly to rise and join in the singing of the *Entrance Song,* which accompanies the *Entrance Procession.* The purpose of the entrance chant or song is to *unify* those gathered into a community so that together they can offer true worship to the Father. GIRM (#39) underlines the importance of the sung prayer of the Church when it says: *"Singing is a sign of the heart's joy." "Whoever sings well, prays twice over."* Ideally, we not only sing the Entrance Song and all the other songs of the Mass but we *pray* them. We *pray* the songs by paying attention to the words and by raising our minds and hearts to God in worship. Often, the Entrance Song has a seasonal theme consistent with the liturgical season of the year. It may also reflect the Scriptures that will be proclaimed in the Liturgy of the Word.

When those involved in the Entrance Procession reach the sanctuary area of the Church, they bow before the altar as a gesture of respect. The deacon places the Book of the Gospels on the altar, which emphasizes the interconnection between the Liturgy of the Word and the Liturgy of the Eucharist. The presider and the deacon *venerate* the altar with a kiss. The Altar-Table symbolizes Christ. The kissing of the altar at the beginning of Mass is an act of greeting to Christ through whom our worship ascends to the Father. The *processional* cross is placed in the sanctuary near the altar to remind us of the intimate connection between the Mass and Calvary. Sometimes the presider *incenses* the altar and the cross as another gesture of respect for these sacred objects. In Christian tradition, the ascending smoke of the incense symbolizes the prayer of our hearts rising up to God: *"Let my prayer be counted as incense before you"* (Ps. 141:2).

Sign of the Cross and Greeting

Presider: In the name of the Father and of the Son and of the Holy Spirit.
People: Amen.
Presider: The Lord be with you.
People: And with your spirit.

After venerating the altar, the presider and the deacon move to the presider's chair. When the *Entrance Song* ends, the presider and assembly join together in making the *Sign of the Cross.* Signing ourselves with the cross reminds us of two basic truths of Christianity, namely, that we begin all things in God the Father, Son and Holy Spirit, and that we are a people saved by the Cross of Christ. When we make the Sign of the Cross, we proclaim that we belong to Christ and that he is our way to the Father. Concerning this gesture, the late Romano Guardini writes: *"When we cross ourselves, let it be with a real sign of the cross...let us make a large, unhurried sign, from forehead to breast, from shoulder to shoulder, consciously feeling how it includes the whole of us.... It is the holiest of all signs"* (Sacred Signs, p.13).

After the Sign of the Cross, the presider formally addresses the assembly in the following words, based on St. Paul's beautiful Trinitarian greeting to the communities he was writing to: *"The grace of our Lord Jesus and the love of God and the communion of the Holy Spirit be with you all,"* or the shorter form: *"The Lord be with you."* The assembly responds: *"And with your spirit."* GIRM states: *"The acclamations and the responses of the faithful, the Priest's greetings and prayers constitute that level of active participation that is to be made by the assembled faithful ... so that the action of the whole community may be expressed and followed"* (35).

In the greeting, the presider and assembly remind each other that the risen Lord Jesus is in their midst, leading them in perfect worship of the Father. In offering the greeting, the presider extends his arms in a gesture of warm welcome to all in the name of Christ. After the greeting, the presider may say a few brief words on the special character of the celebration.

The Penitental Act

In the Gospel of Matthew, Jesus says to us: *"If you bring your gift to the altar and there recall that your brother has anything against you, leave your gift at the altar, go first to be reconciled with your brother and then come and offer your gift"* (5:23-26). In Mark 11:25, Jesus tells us: *"When you stand in prayer, forgive whatever you have against anybody."* The *Penitential Act* is an opportunity for the gathered community to recognize its sinfulness before God and praise God for his mercy. The focus here is not primarily on us and our sins, but rather on Jesus and his mercy. The *Penitential Act* reminds us that we are a community always in need of inner renewal and always in need of God's mercy.

The Penitential Act is usually expressed in one of the following forms:

- ***Confiteor***

  I confess to almighty God,
  and to you, my brothers and sisters,
  that I have greatly sinned,
  in my thoughts and in my words,
  in what I have done, and in what I have failed to do;
  through my fault, through my fault, through my most grievous fault;
  therefore I ask blessed Mary ever-Virgin,
  all the Angels and Saints and you, my brothers and sisters,
  to pray for me to the Lord our God.

In this prayer of contrition, we recognize that we can fail as Christians in four ways: *in our thoughts* (e.g., lust in the heart, judging others); *in our words* (sins of the tongue); *in what we have done* (e.g., selfish, prideful actions); *and in what we have failed to do.* These words remind us that the Christian call is not just about avoiding evil, but also about doing good and growing in self-giving love. In the Gospel, the Rich Young Man (Mt 19:16-24) did a great job at avoiding evil, but failed miserably in doing good, specifically in failing to share his possessions with the poor.

- Another form of the Penitential Act is the Triple Invocation of Christ for his mercy.

  You were sent to heal the contrite. Lord, have mercy.
  You came to call sinners. Christ, have mercy.

You are seated at the right hand of the Father to intercede for us. Lord, have mercy.

- *Sprinkling Rite.* On special occasions, especially during the Easter Season, the Rite of Sprinkling replaces the *Penitential Act.* This *ritual act* reminds us of our Baptism when we were received into God's family, washed clean of sin, and filled with God's life and grace. When the water is sprinkled on us, we make the Sign of the Cross.

Gloria

The Gloria "is a most ancient and venerable hymn by which the Church, gathered in the Holy Spirit, glorifies and entreats God the Father and the Lamb" (GIRM #53). It is a song of joy and praise to God to prepare our hearts and minds to more fully and worthily celebrate the holy mysteries. The opening line of the Gloria (*"Glory to God in the highest"*) is taken from the song of the angels over the fields of Bethlehem when Christ was born (Lk 2:14). (The Gloria is omitted during the penitential seasons of Advent and Lent.)

Collect

In this prayer, the presider with outstretched arms *collects*, as it were, the prayers of the assembly and presents them to God through Jesus by the power of the Holy Spirit. The Collect completes the Introductory Rites of the Mass.

Our behavior at Mass is contagious

When the cantor or song leader invites us to sing the *Entrance Song* we can either respond by opening our hymnal and singing as best we can, or we can ignore the invitation and become silent spectators at Mass. It is important for us to be aware that our behavior at Mass is *contagious.* We can impact those around us in a positive or negative way. When we sing with enthusiasm, pray devoutly, listen intently, show warmth and hospitality, place our money offering in the collection basket, and receive the Body and Blood of Christ with faith and love, we impact in a very positive way the worship atmosphere for those around us. On the other hand, when our presence at Mass is cold, distracted and uninvolved, we diminish the whole worship atmosphere. A powerful example of how our active participation at Mass can impact others is found in the *Confessions of St. Augustine.* Prior to his conversion from his sinful way of life, Augustine would come to church to listen to the homilies and the singing. Concerning the chanting of songs, Augustine writes:

> *How I wept, deeply moved by your hymns, songs, and the voices that echoed through your Church! What emotion I experienced in them! Those sounds flowed into my ears, distilling the truth in my heart. A feeling of devotion surged within me, and tears streamed down my face – tears that did me good.* (CCC #1157)

The prayerful and warm celebration of the Eucharist *attracts* people, while one carried out in a cold and impassive manner is a sure turn-off and *drives* people away. On any given Sunday Mass, we never know how our devout participation or lack of participation is impacting those around us—especially the visitor. Our behavior at Mass may be the reason that a visitor may or may not return.

In the *Constitution of the Sacred Liturgy*, the Vatican II Fathers stated: *"In order that the sacred liturgy may produce its full effect, it is necessary that the faithful come to it with proper dispositions, that their thoughts match their words, and that they cooperate with divine grace lest they receive it in vain"* (#11).

When we gather to celebrate the Eucharist, we must be ready to cooperate with God's grace—grace that will unite us and diminish or even destroy all the harsh, bitter, distrustful and unforgiving attitudes that polarize us. We must make our own Jesus' prayer for unity at the Last Supper: *"I pray that they may be one, as you, Father are in me, and I in you, that they may be one in us, that the world may believe that you sent me"* (John 17:20).

SUMMARY

- The purpose of the *Introductory Rite* is to prepare us to listen to God's Word and to celebrate the Eucharist worthily.
- During Mass, we should not only sing the songs but also *pray* them.
- The *Sign of the Cross* is the holiest of all signs; hence, we should make it slowly and with reverence.
- In the *Penitential Act,* we recognize our sinfulness and we praise God for his mercy. It challenges us to be merciful towards all who have hurt us.

- At Mass, our behavior is contagious. Our active participation in the Mass may touch those around us in ways that we may never know.

QUESTIONS FOR PERSONAL AND GROUP REFLECTION

- What will it demand of you to *pray* the songs at Mass if you are not already doing so?
- Ideally, all of us who participate in the Mass should come with forgiving hearts or with a desire to forgive life's hurts. How challenging is this for you?
- Do you agree that the behavior of others at Mass is contagious? How easy or hard is it for you to sing at Mass if no one is singing around you?

GOOD PRACTICE SUGGESTION

Develop the *good practice* of showing hospitality in Church, aware that the warmth you show to another may be very important to a visitor or to someone who is hurting and feeling alone.

II. LITURGY OF THE WORD

When the Sacred Scriptures are read in church, God himself speaks to his people, and Christ, present in his own Word, proclaims the Gospel. Therefore, all must listen with reverence to the readings from God's Word, for they make up an element of greatest importance in the Liturgy." (GIRM # 29)

In the readings, "the table of God is spread before the faithful, and the treasures of the Bible are opened to them" (GIRM #57).

The Liturgy of the Word consists of:

- First Reading
- Responsorial Psalm
- Second Reading
- Gospel Acclamation

- Gospel
- Homily
- Profession of Faith
- The Universal Prayer

Liturgical calendar with three cycles of readings

The Liturgical Year is the way the Church places before us the main events and teachings in the life of Jesus. Through the liturgical seasons of the year, the Church walks us through the life and mission of Jesus, from prior to his birth to his Ascension into heaven and beyond. In addition to the main seasons of the year (Advent/Christmas, Lent/Easter, Ordinary Time), there are special feast days—like Corpus Christi—and a host of celebrations on the feast days of many of the Saints.

Our Church liturgical calendar has *Three Cycles: A, B, C.* The Gospel reading during *Cycle A* is normally from Matthew, *Cycle B* from Mark, and *Cycle C* from Luke. During the Easter season, the Gospel reading for all three cycles is from John.

For Sunday Masses and on major feasts, there are three readings from Scripture, while weekday Masses have two readings. The readings are proclaimed from the *ambo* (lectern). Just as we are nourished with the Body and Blood of Christ from the *Altar* or the Table of the Eucharist, we are nourished with God's Word from the ambo, the table of God's Word. The assembly is seated in a posture of receptivity and attentiveness. The first and second readings are proclaimed from a book called the *Lectionary* (from *lectio*–to read) and the Gospel passage is proclaimed from the *Book of the Gospels.*

In general, the readings are stories of God's plan to make us his own people. The readings speak of creation, humanity's sin and God's redemption, God's call and our response or failure to respond, our woundedness and God's healing, and God's constant desire to draw us to himself and our resistance to his overtures.

First Reading

The first reading on Sundays and on major feasts is usually from the Old Testament, except during the *Easter Season* when it is from the Acts of the Apostles, which tells us how the Early Christian communities were living witnesses to the Good News of the Resurrection, the focus of the Easter season. The Old Testament Scriptures tell us how God intervened in the long and torturous history of the Israelite people, offering them love and salvation. In these Scriptures, God is gradually revealing himself to his Chosen People. Many of the prophecies of the Old Testament are fulfilled in the New Testament. Writing about the connection between the Old Testament and the New Testament, St. Augustine stated: *"In the Old Testament, the New is hidden; in the New Testament, the Old appears."*

The first reading is chosen to *connect* with the Gospel in some way. The connection between the Old Testament passage and the Gospel passage is not always clear and could easily be missed. Some-times the connection is one of *prophecy fulfillment*—what was prophesied in the Old Testament is fulfilled in the New Testament. Other times, the linkage is one of *contrast*. The first reading may be about the negative attitude towards lepers and sinners and, in contrast, the Gospel may speak of Jesus' mercy and care for the outcast and sinner.

At the end of the first and second readings, the reader says: *"The Word of the Lord,"* and the assembly responds: *"Thanks be to God."* By this reply, "the assembled people give honor to the Word of God that they have received in faith and with gratitude" (GIRM #59). Ideally, our *"Thanks be to God"* should be a great shout reminding us how wonderful it is to hear God speak to us through the Scriptures.

Silence

Several times during Mass are moments for silent prayer. For instance, during the Liturgy of the Word, a moment of silence is observed after the first and second readings, and again after the homily. Concerning the importance of liturgical silence, the U.S. Bishops' Committee on the Liturgy has these beautiful words to share with us.

> *Liturgical silence is not merely an absence of words, a pause, or an interlude. Rather, it is a stillness, a quieting of spirits, a taking of time and leisure to hear, assimilate, and respond. Any haste that hinders reflectiveness should be avoided. The dialogue between God and the community of faith taking place through the Holy Spirit requires intervals of silence, suited to the congregation, so that all can take to heart the Word of God and respond to it in prayer. (Introduction of the Mass #48)*

The Responsorial Psalm

The psalm, which follows the first reading, is called *responsorial* because it is a prayer (ideally, a sung prayer) of *response* to the

Word of God that we just heard in the first reading. The psalm usually echoes some thought expressed in the first reading. In his book *Mystery of Faith,* Lawrence Johnson writes: *"The responsorial psalm is not just a response to the reading.... It also helps the gathered assembly create an atmosphere of prayer, one in which all can recall what God has done and continues to do. To a certain extent the psalm serves as a meditative prolongation of the readings, offering us through poetry a rich opportunity to savor the Word of God"* (p.36).

Second Reading

The second reading is always taken from one of the letters in the New Testament or from the Book of Revelation. The reading may be a teaching on some issue or it may address a pastoral problem. It gives us a glimpse into the attempts of the early Christians to follow the ways of Christ. Though there might seem to be a connection between the second reading and the first reading or the Gospel, this was not the intention of the compilers of the lectionary. In Ordinary Time, the second reading is a semi-continuous passage from one of the Epistles. During the major seasons and feasts, the second reading is chosen to harmonize with the other readings.

Gospel Acclamation and Gospel

The proclamation of the Gospel is the climactic moment of the Liturgy of the Word as it is always about Christ and what he has said and done. During the *Gospel Acclamation* and the *Gospel,* we stand as an outward expression of joy for the Good News that we are about to hear. It is also a mark of respect for Jesus who is about to address us. (The word Gospel means Good News.)

The Gospel Acclamation, chanted prior to the Gospel, is a hymn of joy which accompanies the Gospel procession. The Book of the Gospels, which has been placed on the altar or on a special stand at the beginning of Mass, is now brought in procession to the ambo, accompanied by two candle bearers. Sometimes, the presider or the deacon incenses the Gospel before it is proclaimed. The joyful chanting, the procession with candles and incense, are all intended to highlight for us the supreme importance of what is about to take place, namely, Jesus addressing us.

Before the deacon proclaims the Gospel, he receives a blessing from the presider who quietly prays, *"May the Lord be in your heart and on your lips that you may proclaim his Gospel worthily and well, in the name of the Father and of the Son and of the Holy Spirit."* Before the Gospel is proclaimed, all present make a threefold Sign of the Cross on their forehead, lips and heart. While no official commentary on the Mass explains the meaning of this gesture, it is sometimes taught as a prayer in which we say "may the Lord be in my *mind* that I may know the Word of God, and on my *lips* that I may speak the Word of God, and in my *heart* that I may love the Word of God." When the deacon has finished, he kisses the Book of the Gospels as a mark of loving respect, and softly says: *"Through the words of the Gospel, may our sins be wiped away."*

During the proclamation of the readings, our primary challenge is to be an *active listener* to allow God's Word to speak to our hearts. This is especially trying if we are self-preoccupied, if the reader does a poor job of proclaiming the Word, or if the readings are difficult to understand. In this *age of noise,* when we have become adept at tuning out the barrage of words coming at us all day long, it may be particularly difficult for us to hear words written thousands of years ago to another people living at a time very different from ours. Each Sunday, we must make a deliberate decision to open our hearts to hear God's message. We need to pray for a *Mary-heart,* a heart that is receptive and responsive to God. We might pray: *"Lord, cleanse my heart of all obstacles that block me from hearing your Word. May my heart be rich soil where your Word can bear fruit a hundred fold."*

Homily

The late French liturgist, Father Lucien Deiss, describes the aim of the homilist in this way: *"The homilist must show this particular congregation how the Word they have just heard is relevant to their lives. He helps them to hear Christ's voice and see Christ's face in the sacred text. The homilist leads the assembly to look at itself, its joys, its sorrows, its problems, and judge them in the light of God's Word."* In other words, a good homily will link the life of the assembly with the readings just proclaimed. A good homily both encourages and challenges. It comforts the afflicted and afflicts the comfortable.

Drawing from my own experience, the following are four practical ways that the assembly can help priests and deacons in their ministry of preaching.

- *Pray* that God's Spirit may guide the homilist in delivering a homily that will be truly Good News for all who hear it.

- *Pray* for the *assembly* that they may have open and receptive hearts, and that they may hear the Word God wants them to hear on this particular Sunday.
- As the homily is being delivered, try to be an *active and attentive listener.* Our attentiveness and expectancy help to draw the best from the homilist. On the contrary, nothing can discourage the best-intentioned homilist more than an assembly of faces that are expressionless, distracted and seemingly just wanting to get through the Mass as quickly as possible.
- Consider making *constructive suggestions* to the homilist especially if you are someone who takes the time to give positive feedbacks. Suggestions for improvement should be within the capability of the homilist.
- Finally, a word of caution. Many of us need to be aware of any attitude or feeling of indifference we may harbor towards a certain priest or deacon because we do not like his personality or his liturgical style, or because we have decided that God cannot speak to us through him. If God was able to speak to Balaam through his donkey (Num 22:22-35), surely he can speak to us through priests or deacons however poor or unworthy they may be as his spokesmen. There is no homily so bad that we cannot get at least one idea from it for our lives.

After the homily, there is another period of *silent reflection,* the purpose of which is to give us the time to be still with the Word and to ask ourselves: What does the Word mean for my life? What *action* is required of me so that the Word just proclaimed and preached becomes a living Word in my life? *"Lord, you just spoke to me. What do you want me to hear? What do you want me to answer? Speak, Lord, your servant is listening."*

Catechumens and Candidates – Rite of Dismissal

Catechumens are unbaptized persons who are seeking Baptism and entrance into our Catholic community. *Candidates* are baptized persons raised in another Christian faith-tradition who are seeking Full Communion with our Catholic community. In most parishes today, after the homily at one of the weekend Masses, these brothers and sisters are called forth, prayed over and sent forth to reflect more fully on the readings just proclaimed. In the Church's initiation process, this is called the *Rite of Dismissal.* Since they cannot yet participate in Holy Communion, they are sent forth to be further nourished by reflecting together on the Word of God. While it is not normative practice to dismiss *baptized candidates* from the liturgy, it is, however, a common pastoral practice in parishes. In such cases, it is believed that reflection on the Scriptures (with the Catechumens) is a necessary element of their formation.

Profession of Faith (Creed)

Having listened to the Word of God in the readings, the community rises to give public witness to the faith of our Baptism. The *Nicene* Creed which we profess was composed in the fourth century in the course of two Church councils: Nicaea in 325 and Constantinople in 381. These Councils were called to combat heresies that defied the doctrine of the Blessed Trinity. The Nicene Creed expresses true doctrine concerning our belief in the three distinct persons in one God. For 2,000 years, the Church has protected and defended her identity as *one, holy, catholic and apostolic* by living and dying by the words of the Nicene Creed.

The big danger today is the tendency for many of us to profess our faith (recite the Creed) in a thoughtless, mechanical way, not mindful of the thousands who died willingly rather than deny their faith in God the Father, Son and Holy Spirit. We in the free world may forget our brothers and sisters in other parts of the world who are still persecuted for their Christian faith. In her excellent book, *The Mass, its Rituals, Roots and Relevance in our Lives*, Joan Carter McHugh writes: *"Each Sunday, when we stand up to say, 'We believe in one God, the Father Almighty...,' we join the millions of our ancestors who have gone ahead of us, entering into a great current that will flow until the end of time. How blessed we are to be able to stand up in church, step into that current, joining millions of Christ's disciples, past and present, who gratefully live and willingly die, by the words of the Nicene Creed."*

The Universal Prayer

Enlightened and moved by God's Word, all the baptized now share in the priestly intercession of Christ for all humanity. The gathered assembly of believers prays for the needs of the Church, for civil authorities, for the oppressed, and for the local community, especially the sick and the dead.

Concerning the power and importance of intercessory prayer, the late Fr. Anthony de Mello, S.J., writes: *"It is only at the end of this world that we shall realize how the destinies of persons and nations have been shaped, not so much by the external actions of powerful men and by events that seemed inevitable, but by the quiet, silent, irresistible prayer of persons the world will never know."*

Our concern for others expands our hearts and directs our love outside of ourselves. This prayer gives us the opportunity to bring local and global needs before the throne of God, trusting that his response is always in our best interest.

SUMMARY

- When the Scriptures are proclaimed in Church, God himself is speaking to us.
- The Scripture readings speak of humanity's sin and God's redemption, God's call and our response or lack of response, and God's constant desire to draw us to himself.
- Liturgical silence gives us the opportunity to assimilate the Word that we have just heard.
- The purpose of the homily is to lead the assembly to look at itself, its joys and sorrows in the light of God's Word.
- The Creed expresses true doctrine concerning our belief in the three distinct persons of the Blessed Trinity.
- The Universal Prayer or Prayer of the Faithful, is our opportunity to share in Christ's intercession for our Church, civil authorities and other local and global needs.

QUESTIONS FOR PERSONAL AND GROUP REFLECTION

- To what extent are you aware or spiritually awake to the fact that during the Liturgy of the Word, God himself is addressing us? What might help us to grow in our appreciation of this great truth?
- What do you look for in a homily?
- What can help us from reciting the Creed in a mechanical way?

GOOD PRACTICE SUGGESTION

Develop the *good practice* of going over the Sunday readings alone or with a small group before attending Sunday Mass. A process for doing this is available on the author's parish website: www.ascensioncatholic.net (on homepage, click on Fr. Tobin's Writings, then scroll down to Sunday Readings. In this resource, you will find a commentary on each of the Sunday readings as well as reflection questions that you can use alone or with others.)

III. LITURGY OF THE EUCHARIST

"At the last Supper, Christ instituted the Paschal Sacrifice and banquet, by which the Sacrifice of the Cross is continuously made present in the Church whenever the Priest, representing Christ the Lord, carries out what the Lord himself did and handed over to his disciples to be done in his memory." (GIRM #72)

In the Liturgy of the Word, the wonderful works of God are proclaimed. Our response to that proclamation is one of gratitude which we offer to God in the Liturgy of the Eucharist. The focus of our attention moves from the ambo to the Altar-Table.

The Liturgy of the Eucharist has three sub-sections:

- Preparation of the Altar and the Presentation of the Gifts
- Eucharistic Prayer
- Communion Rite

During the Liturgy of the Eucharist, we ritualize *four actions* that Jesus did at the Last Supper.

- Jesus *took bread and wine* = the presider takes the gifts of bread and wine from the representatives of the assembly (Presentation of the Gifts).
- Jesus *gave thanks* = we offer our great prayer of thanksgiving to our heavenly Father (Eucharistic Prayer).
- Jesus *broke bread* = the large host is broken into many parts prior to Holy Communion (Breaking of Bread).
- Jesus *gave it to them* = the assembly receives the bread and wine which have been transformed into the Body and Blood of Christ (Holy Communion).

During the Liturgy of the Eucharist, we pray that our lives may be *taken, blessed, broken* and made ready to *share* with others. As we receive the Eucharist, we pray that our lives may become Eucharist for others.

The purpose of the Preparation of the Altar and the Presentation of the Gifts is to let all present know that the Eucharistic offering is about to begin.

Preparation of the Altar

In this simple ritual, the assembly's focus is moved from the ambo to the *Altar-Table* where our Eucharistic Jesus comes to us. *"The altar-table is at one and the same time both a table of sacrifice and the table of the paschal banquet, a unique* ***altar*** *on which the sacrifice* *of the cross is perpetuated in mystery until Christ comes, and a* ***table*** *at which the Church's children assemble to give thanks to God and receive the Body and Blood of Christ"* (Dedication of a Church and an Altar ch. 4, #4).

When Martin Luther denied the *sacrificial* aspect of the Mass, the Church took great pains to emphasize it, so much so that she almost lost sight of the *meal or banquet* aspect. Since Vatican II, the Church has emphasized both aspects. When the early Christians celebrated Mass, they were aware that Jesus, their *risen brother,* the same Jesus who was the *slain Lamb of God* (Rev 5:12) who poured out his life for the forgiveness of sin, was in their midst. We also note that the very language of the institution narrative (the words of Jesus at the last Supper) is *sacrificial.* It speaks of a *body to be broken* and *blood to be poured out.* For Jesus, the reality of what was to happen the next day on Calvary was part of the meal that he was celebrating with his Apostles. For Jesus, his sacrifice on the Cross was an act of total self-surrender to the Father. At the Mass we re-link, as it were, ourselves to the Paschal mystery of Jesus. Saint Paul told his converts in Corinth: *"Every time you eat this bread and drink this cup, you proclaim the death of the Lord until he comes"* (1Cor 11:26).

The deacon or a lay minister prepares the altar by lighting two candles (if not already lit), then places on the altar a white cloth called a corporal, the Roman Missal, and the sacred vessels.

Presentation of the Gifts

During this ritual, representatives of the assembly bring forward in procession the gifts of bread and wine, and the money offering.

It is also appropriate for the members of the assembly to bring forward food for the poor (GIRM #73). This action reminds us of the intimate connection between the Eucharist and our call to share our bread with the poor. The Eucharistic gifts come in the form of bread and wine because not only did Jesus himself use them but also because they are universal symbols of food and unity. Just as many grapes are pressed to make wine, and many grains of wheat are crushed to make bread, many people come as one family to praise God in joyful, loving celebration. The bread is unleavened, not our usual bread but a simple bread, the bread of the poor. *"In this bread we cast our lot with the poor, knowing ourselves – however materially affluent – to be poor people, needy and hungry. Unless we acknowledge our hunger, we have no place at this table. How else can God feed us?"* (Joseph Cardinal Bernardin)

Our money offering symbolizes our hours of hard work, which we now offer to God in the Presentation of the Gifts. Here, we bring, as it were, our entire lives and all our little sacrifices to Jesus who is represented by the priest.

After receiving the gifts of bread and wine, the presider prays over them using a blessing prayer which has its roots in Jewish blessings over bread and wine.

Blessed are you, Lord God of all creation,
for through your goodness we have received the bread we offer you:
fruit of the earth and work of human hands,
it will become for us the bread of life.

Blessed are you, Lord God of all creation,
for through your goodness we have received the wine we offer you:

fruit of the vine and work of human hands,
it will become our spiritual drink.

Mixing of water and wine

The *mixing of a little water with the wine* reflects a table practice in the days of Jesus. Later on, an incarnational symbolism was attached to the rite. As the presider pours a little water (symbolizing weak humanity) and wine (symbolizing the divinity of Christ) into the chalice, he silently prays: *"By the mystery of this water and wine, may we come to share in the divinity of Christ who humbled himself to share in our humanity."* When the gifts of bread and wine have been prepared, the presider invokes a prayer of blessing over each one, referring to them as the *work of our hands* which reminds us of the sacredness of human labor performed in the name of God, and thus a source of holiness.

At this time, the altar and gifts may be *incensed* as a sign of the Church's offering and prayer rising to God. The presider and people are also incensed since they are to unite themselves and their prayers with the gifts of bread and wine, which will become the Body and Blood of Christ during the Eucharistic Prayer.

Washing of the hands

In the early centuries, the washing of the hands may have had a practical function. After receiving gifts of food for the poor, the presider's hands were soiled and in need of washing. Today, the gesture has a symbolic value in that the presider asks God to cleanse his heart before he offers the sacrifice of Christ. He silently prays from Psalm 51: *"Wash me, O Lord, from my iniquity, cleanse me of my sin."*

The presider then invites the assembly to: *"Pray, brethren (brothers and sisters), that my sacrifice and yours may be acceptable to God, the Almighty Father."* The words *"my sacrifice and yours"* are important because they remind us that at Mass, *all* present are celebrants because of Baptism (1Pet 2:9). We are a celebrating community within which there are different functions or ministries.

The assembly responds: *"May the Lord accept the sacrifice at your hands for the praise and glory of his name, for our good and the good of all his holy Church"*—which calls to mind the twofold purpose of the Eucharistic sacrifice: the glory of God and the ongoing sanctification of his people.

Prayer over the Offerings

Prayer over the Offerings is a petition to God to accept our gifts with joyful anticipation of the transformation of the bread and wine into the Body and Blood of Christ. *Prayer over the Offerings* concludes the section on *Preparation of the Altar and Presentation of the Gifts.*

SUMMARY

- During the Liturgy of the Eucharist, we give praise and worship for the wonderful works of God, especially for creation and our redemption in Christ.
- During this part of the Mass, we prepare the altar and the gifts of bread and wine brought forward by members of the assembly.

QUESTIONS FOR PERSONAL AND GROUP REFLECTION

- Our Church tells us that the Eucharist is a sacred meal and *sacrifice*. What does this mean to you?
- Does your parish bring forward food for the poor during Mass? If so, what meaning does this action have for you? Can you see how participation in the Eucharist calls us to share our bread with the hungry?

GOOD PRACTICE SUGGESTION

As the gifts are brought forward, develop the *good practice* of presenting the work of your hands to the Lord. Also consider bringing to Church food for the poor.

Eucharistic Prayer

The Eucharistic Prayer is "the center and summit of the entire celebration." (GIRM #78)

It is essentially a statement of praise and thanksgiving, a proclamation of wonder for God's work of salvation as well as an action that makes the Eucharist, rendering present both the Body and Blood of the Lord and the Lord's great redeeming action. (The Mystery of Faith, p.74)

During the Eucharistic Prayer, the Body and Blood of Christ are made present by the power of the Holy Spirit, and the people of God are joined to Christ in offering his sacrifice to the Father. The people participate in this great prayer and profess their faith in what is happening through the chanting of several acclamations. On any given Sunday, the presider prays one of ten Eucharistic Prayers.

Preface

The Eucharistic Prayer opens with a thanksgiving prayer called the *Preface*. It starts with a dialogue between the presider and the assembly in which all present are urged to *lift up their hearts and give thanks to God for the wonderful gifts of creation, redemption and sanctification.* The phrase "lift up our hearts" is an invitation *"to place in God's presence our entire being, thoughts, memories, emotions and expectations, in grateful attention and anticipation"* (Introduction to the Mass, p.85). Today, the Church has over 80 prefaces. While all the prefaces have the same basic structure, each one reflects a liturgical season, feast day, or special occasion.

Because this part of the Mass is basically the same each Sunday, there is a real danger that we tune out and become mentally absent. It takes a real effort on our part to stay focused on the awesome action that is about to take place. During the Eucharistic Prayer, we are summoned to leave behind all our concerns and to lift up our spirits in contemplation of the great mystery about to be accomplished. In addition, the faithful exercise their baptismal priesthood by participating in the singing or reciting of three acclamations.

Acclamation ("Holy, Holy, Holy")

In the *Sanctus* acclamation (*"Holy, Holy, Holy"*), all present join their voices to all of creation in giving glory to God with words inspired by the vision of Isaiah (Is 6:3). In each celebration of the Eucharist, the Church is taken up into the eternal liturgy in which the entire communion of saints, the heavenly powers, and all of creation, give praise to the God of the universe.

Speaking of the presence of angels during Mass, St. Brigid writes:

> *One day while I was assisting at the Holy Sacrifice, I saw an immense number of holy Angels descend and gather around the altar contemplating the priest. They sang heavenly canticles and ravished my heart; heaven itself seemed to be contemplating the great sacrifice. And yet we poor blind miserable creatures assist at Mass with so little love, relish and*

respect. Oh! If God would open our eyes what wonders should we not see. (All About Angels, Fr. Paul O'Sullivan, O.P.)

Epiclesis

The Eucharistic Prayer now continues with the *Epiclesis,* a Greek word for *"calling down upon."* The *Catechism of the Catholic Church* (1105) explains what happens during the *Epiclesis*: *"The Epiclesis (invocation upon) is the intercession in which the priest begs the Father to send the Holy Spirit, the Sanctifier, so that the offerings may become the Body and Blood of Christ and that the faithful, by receiving them, may themselves become a living offering to God."* The *Epiclesis* portion of Eucharistic Prayer II is expressed as follows:

You are indeed holy, O Lord, the fount of all holiness.
Make holy, therefore, these gifts, we pray,
by sending down your Spirit upon them like the dewfall,
so that they may become for us the Body and Blood
of our Lord Jesus Christ.

An early Father of the Church, St. John Damascene, writes: *"If anyone wishes to know how the bread is changed into the Body of Christ at Mass, I will tell him. The Holy Spirit overshadows the priest and acts on him as he acted on the Blessed Virgin Mary, when the angel Gabriel visited her."*

The Institution Narrative/Consecration

The *Institution Narrative* contains the words Jesus used at the

Last Supper over the bread and wine. Concerning this mystery of our faith, the *United States Catholic Catechism for Adults* (p.223) states:

> *Since the Middle Ages, the change of bread and wine into the Body and Blood of Christ has been called "transubstantiation." This means that the substance of the bread and wine is changed into the substance of the Body and Blood of Christ. The appearances of bread and wine remain (color, shape, weight, chemical composition), but the underlying reality – that is, the substance – is now the Body and Blood of Christ.*

In his sacrifice on the Cross, Christ totally poured out his life for us, totally letting go of himself that we might live and be reconciled to God and each other. Jesus seeks to draw us into his act of total self-giving so that we might give of ourselves in service to others. If we find it a challenge to believe that Jesus is truly present in the bread and wine at Mass, we would do well to meditate on these wise words of St. Cyril of Alexandria:

> *Do not doubt whether this is true, but rather receive the words of our Savior in faith, for since he is the truth, he cannot lie. (CCC #1381)*

"For many or for all." In the previous translation of the words of Consecration, the presider proclaimed that Jesus poured out his life *"for all."* The new translation states that Jesus poured out his life "for many." Does this mean that Jesus did not die for all people? Two things to note here: (1) the new translation is closer to the biblical text (Mt 26:28); (2) Jesus did die for all, but not all choose to accept Jesus' offer of salvation. Each of us must choose to accept Jesus' gift and follow his teachings so that we can be counted amongst "the many."

Memorial Acclamation

After the words of Consecration, the Memorial Acclamation is said or sung. This is our shout of joy and thanks to Christ, whose memory we keep and who will one day return to take us home. When the presider says, *"The mystery of faith,"* he is expressing his profound wonder at what has just taken place. In and through one of the acclamations, the faithful exercise their baptismal priesthood and actively participate in the Eucharistic Prayer.

Anamenesis

Anamnesis is a Greek word meaning *"remembering."* In the context of Jewish and Catholic liturgy, *Anamnesis* is a remembering that *makes present today* an event that occurred in the past. While the whole Eucharistic Prayer is, in a real sense, an anamnesis or re-calling, it especially refers to these words in the Eucharistic Prayer:

> *Therefore, O Lord, as we celebrate the memorial*
> *of the saving Passion of your Son,*
> *his wondrous Resurrection and Ascension into heaven,*
> *and as we look forward to his second coming,*
> *we offer you in thanksgiving this holy and living sacrifice.*

As stated above, *"calling to mind"* is not just remembering what

Jesus did 2,000 years ago. It is rather a *re-actuating—"a re-presentation before God of the saving deeds that he has accomplished in Christ so that their fullness and power may be effective here and now"* (Introduction to the Mass #121, CCC #1366). A past event becomes a *now event.* In human experience, perhaps the closest we can get to understanding *Anamnesis* is when we tell stories about a deceased loved one who, in a real sense, becomes present to us.

Oblations

Following the *Anamnesis,* and closely related to it, is the prayer of oblation. GIRM (#79) tells us that in the prayer of oblation, *"the Church and in particular the Church here and now gathered – offers in the Holy Spirit the spotless Victim to the Father...."* The same paragraph of GIRM exhorts that *"the faithful not only offer this spotless Victim but also learn to offer themselves, and so day by day to be consummated, through Christ the Mediator, into unity with God and with each other, so that at last God may be all in all."*

During this part of the Eucharistic Prayer, we make our own the sacrifice of Christ. This is the moment for us to unite our sufferings and trials to those of Christ. Each Eucharistic Prayer expresses the *Oblation* in a slightly different way. Eucharistic Prayer III states it in this way:

Look, we pray, upon the oblation of your Church
and, recognizing the sacrificial Victim
by whose death you willed to reconcile us to yourself,
grant that we, who are nourished by the Body and Blood of your Son

and filled with his Holy Spirit,
may become one body, one spirit in Christ.

Intercessions

Near the end of the Eucharistic Prayer, the presider presents the intercessory prayers for a variety of causes and people: the deceased, the universal Church, the Pope, the local bishop, the clergy, and all the people of God.

As we join ourselves to the perfect offering of Christ to the Father, we also join ourselves to all of the faithful—both living and dead. We pray that the salvation gained by Jesus be experienced by all. In the Eucharist, earth unites itself with heaven. We join our prayer to the perfect prayer of Jesus. As we do so, we remember those who have gone ahead of us, especially Mary, St. Joseph, the Apostles and all the saints. We also remember our spiritual leaders here on earth and all the faithful, especially those gathered to celebrate this particular Eucharist.

Doxology

Doxology means hymn of praise. During this shout of praise to our triune God, the presider lifts up the chalice and host, and chants or says:

Through him, with him, in him,
O God, almighty Father,

in the unity of the Holy Spirit,
all glory and honor is yours,
for ever and ever.

So the Eucharistic Prayer ends as it begins—with a shout of praise and thanks to God. The assembly responds by singing the *Great Amen.* It is the most important acclamation of the whole Mass. *Amen* means *"so be it."* It is our *YES* to all that has been done and proclaimed. It is our burst of praise to our God who has done such wonderful things for us. The *Great Amen* brings the Eucharistic prayer to its completion.

SUMMARY

- The Eucharist Prayer is the high point of the Liturgy of the Eucharist when the bread and wine become the Body and Blood of Christ.
- During the Eucharistic Prayer, earth unites with heaven in giving praise to God.
- The same Holy Spirit who overshadowed Mary and empowered her to conceive Jesus, overshadows the priest at Mass and empowers him to change the bread and wine into the Body and Blood of Christ.
- The Eucharistic Prayer ends with a shout of praise to our God who blesses us in so many ways.

QUESTIONS FOR PERSONAL AND GROUP REFLECTION

- What helps you *not* to mentally check out during this part of the Mass?
- It is not uncommon for people to suffer from doubts about Jesus' presence in the Eucharist. Has this been an issue for you? If so, what has helped you to deal with it?

GOOD PRACTICE SUGGESTION

Develop the *good practice* of offering your whole life, your joys and sorrows, to Christ during the Eucharist Prayer.

Communion Rite

The banquet of the Lord is ready. All present now prepare themselves to receive the Body and Blood of Christ. Holy Communion at Mass is an expression of our unity with Christ and with all of God's people. It is the culmination of our Eucharistic celebration.

The prayers and rituals during this section of the Mass are intended to prepare us to receive Jesus, our Savior and Lord, in Holy Communion.

The Lord's Prayer

In the Lord's Prayer, we as a community address God as *Our Father* (our *Papa*, as Jesus referred to him). Our relationship is not to be one of fear but one of love. We use Matthew's version (6:9-13) of the Lord's Prayer—not Luke 11:2-4—as it is richer and fuller, containing a larger number of petitions.

The Lord's Prayer has two petitions that make it a particularly appropriate prayer in preparation for the reception of Holly Communion, i.e., 1) *"Give us our daily bread,"* and 2) *"Forgive us our trespasses as we forgive those who trespass against us." Daily bread* is the Bread of Life we receive in Communion. As for *forgiveness,* we are reminded of the importance of approaching the Eucharist with a forgiving heart, or a heart that sincerely desires to forgive.

The final petition in the Lord's Prayer is *"Deliver us from evil"*—to which the presider adds a beautiful invocation asking God to protect us from sin and evil, and to grant us his peace *"as we wait in joyful hope for the coming of his kingdom."* We Christians are involved in a spiritual warfare (Eph 6:10-17) against an enemy that is the subtlest of all creatures (Gen 3:1); hence, we often need to pray for deliverance like this great prayer said at every Mass.

The Rite of Peace

The Rite of Peace begins with this beautiful prayer:

Lord Jesus Christ, who said to your Apostles,
"Peace I leave you, my peace I give you,"

look not on our sins, but on the faith of your Church,
and graciously grant her peace and unity
in accordance with your will.

In this prayer, the presider addresses Jesus, recalling his words at the Last Supper: *"Peace I leave you, my peace, I give you"* (Jn 14:27). The peace Jesus offers is deeper than the peace that comes when the internal circumstances of our lives are going well, e.g., good health, financial security, good relationships. As we know, all these blessings can go away overnight.

The peace Jesus offers comes from a strong relationship with him and can sustain us even when the external circumstances of our lives are not good. This is the peace we offer to those around us at this part of the Mass. The gesture acknowledges that Christ whom we receive in the Sacrament is already present in our neighbor, and expresses our sincere desire to forgive all hurts and to be at peace with all people.

Breaking of the Bread

The presider takes the large host and breaks it into many parts. The meaning of this ritual is beautifully explained to us by St. Paul in his first letter to the Church at Corinth: *"The bread that we break, is it not a participation in the body of Christ? Because the loaf of bread is one, we, though many, are one body, for we all partake of the loaf"* (10:16-17). Despite its rich diversity, the Church is one as it gathers to celebrate our unity in Christ (Mystery of Faith, p.104).

Reflecting on the ritual of the breaking of bread, Fr. Cantalamesso, a preacher to the papal household says:

> *To understand this ritual, I must, first of all, 'break' myself... Lay before God all hardness, all rebellion towards him or towards others, crush my pride, submit and say 'yes' fully to all that God asks of me. I too must repeat the words: Lo, I have come to do thy will, O God! You don't want many things from me; you want me and I say 'yes.' To be Eucharist like Jesus signifies being totally abandoned to the Father's will."* (Quoted in The Mass, p.226)

Commingling Rite

In the *Breaking of the Bread*, the presider places a small portion of the host in the chalice to *"signify the unity of the Body and Blood of the Lord in the work of salvation"* (GIRM #83). This comingling of the consecrated elements is an expression of our belief that the Body of Christ is not without the Blood of Christ, and the Blood of Christ is not without the Body of Christ, i.e., Christ is totally present in *both* the bread and wine.

The assembly sings or recites a short litany (*Agnus Dei* or Lamb of God): *"Lamb of God, who takes away the sins of the world, have mercy on us."* In his first letter, Peter reminds us that we are *"saved, not with perishable things like silver or gold but with the precious Blood of Christ as of a spotless, unblemished lamb"* (1Pet 1:18).

Communion

The presider and the people take a solemn moment to prepare

themselves to receive Holy Communion. One of two prayers that the presider prays quietly at this time is the following:

May the receiving of your Body and Blood, Lord Jesus Christ,
not bring me to judgment and condemnation,
but through your loving mercy
be for me protection in mind and body
and a healing remedy.

Invitation to Holy Communion

Holding the large host above the chalice, the presider says:

Behold the Lamb of God!
Behold him who takes away the sins of the world.
Blessed are those called to the Supper of the Lamb.

"Behold the Lamb of God..." are the words used by John the Baptist (Jn 1:29) when he saw Jesus during his baptism ministry at the Jordan.

The assembly responds:

Lord, I am not worthy that you should enter under my roof
but only say the Word and my soul will be healed.

These are the words spoken by the Roman centurion when he asked Jesus to heal his servant (Mt 8:8). The centurion is a model of faith, humility and confidence for all of us waiting to receive Jesus, the Lamb of God, in Holy Communion.

In an effort to draw out the deep meaning of the Lord's invitation and the symbolism of the Eucharist, catechist and teacher Marie McIntyre writes:

> *When the priest takes the bread and wine into his hands and elevates them for all to see, it is as if Christ is calling out to us and saying:*
>
> *"Here I am present in your midst under forms of life—bread and wine—to remind you that I am your life and you will have life forever if you come to me and learn from me to love the Father as I do.*
>
> *Here I am bread and wine to be shared—eaten—consumed so that I may become part of you, enter into your life and sustain you.*
>
> *Here I am as a total gift—as a sign that to be like me, you have to be ready to give yourselves for others. Here I am sharing symbols of life and joy because I want you to live my life and share my joy.*
>
> *Here I am as a sign of life freely given, freely shared so that all might come and none be turned away. Here I am for you because I love you."*

Proper disposition for receiving Holy Communion

When it comes to receiving Holy Communion, we should remember the words of St. Paul: *"Whoever therefore eats the bread and drinks the cup of the Lord in an unworthy manner will be guilty of profaning the Body and Blood of the Lord"* (1Cor 11:27). With *these* words in mind, we can say that *two extremes* are to be avoided. If we suffer from an overly *scrupulous conscience,* we might judge ourselves as never worthy of Holy Communion unless we have received the Sacrament of Reconciliation the day before. Such a scrupulous conscience brands God as a very demanding task-master who is never satisfied with us. In contrast, some people might casually approach the Table of the Lord without regard to their spiritual state as, for instance, when they carry a hard-ened heart that absolutely refuses to forgive a hurt or to pray for the grace of forgiveness. The *United States Catholic Catechism for Adults* reminds us that we should conscientiously prepare for the moment of Holy Communion. *"We should be in the state of grace, and if we are conscious of a grave or serious sin, we must receive the Sacrament of Penance before receiving Holy Communion. We are also expected to fast from food and drink for at least one hour prior to the reception of Holy Communion"* (p.222). Even though none of us is worthy to receive our Divine Lord in Holy Communion (*Lord, I am not worthy . . . .*), all of us must make every effort to be the least unworthy that we can be.

Communion Procession

After the presider, deacons, and extraordinary ministers of the bread and cup receive the Body and Blood of Christ and arrive at their communion stations, members of the assembly process to the stations closest to them to receive our Divine Lord. Our Church tells us that it is desirable that all who are in a state of grace receive both the Body *and* the Blood of Christ. By doing so, the *sign of the Eucharistic banquet* is more clearly evident (GIRM # 281). In ministering the host and the cup, the presider, deacon or extraordinary minister says: *"Body of Christ"* or *"Blood of Christ,"* as appropriate. On our part, we bow slightly before we take the bread and cup (an act of reverence for our Divine Lord), then respond: *"Amen" (Yes, I believe that you are fully present in the bread and cup).*

Communion is a great moment of intimacy between the Lord and the members of his body. We come forward, not as isolated individuals, but as brothers and sisters in Christ. We come forward, not in a sluggish way, but with reverence and love for him who is the life of the world. By exclaiming our Amen to the minister's words: "The Body of Christ," we are really proclaiming:

I believe, Jesus, that you are the Bread of Life.
I believe, Jesus, that you are the power that can transform my life.
I believe that these people are my brothers and sisters and part of the one Body of Christ.
I accept, Jesus, the challenge to become your bread for others and to build up your Body in the world.

In the hand or on the tongue?

We have the option of receiving Communion in the hand or on the tongue. Many Catholics who were raised in the pre-Vatican II Church think that receiving Holy Communion in the hand was a Vatican II initiative. It is not. Though we do not know for certain, we can safely assume that the Apostles at the Last Supper received the bread in their hands from Jesus. We also know that back in the first millennium, Catholic Christians usually received Communion in their hand. St. Cyril of Jerusalem describes the fourth century practice in this way:

When you approach, do not go stretching out your hands or having your fingers spread out, but make the left hand into a throne for the right one, which shall receive the King, and then cup your open hand and take the Body of Christ, reciting the Amen.

During the distribution of Holy Communion, an appropriate hymn is sung. Our participation in the singing of the Communion hymn expresses our spiritual union with all communicants. When we return to our pew after receiving Holy Communion, we should continue to join in the singing rather than engage in our own private prayer.

Fruits and implications of receiving Holy Communion

The Catechism of the Catholic Church (#1391-1401) tells us of the many different fruits we receive with Holy Communion.

Holy Communion augments our union with Christ (#1391)
The principal fruit of receiving Holy Communion is the intimate union with Christ. In his discourse on the Bread of Life, Jesus says: "He who eats my flesh and drinks my blood abides in me and I in him" (6:56). Paul sees this abiding in terms of putting on Christ, identifying with Christ, developing within ourselves Christ's outlook, attitudes and his commitment to the Father. Unless we abide in Christ, all our efforts are in vain (Jn 15:4). Hence, receiving Holy Communion entails a willingness to do all we can to have the same attitude that is also ours in Christ Jesus (Phi 2:5).

Holy Communion separates us from sin (#1393)
The Catechism states: "The Body of Christ we receive in Holy

Communion is 'given up for us' and the Blood we drink 'shed for the many for the forgiveness of sins.' For this reason the Eucharist cannot unite us to Christ without at the same time cleansing us from past sins and preserving us from future sins." This teaching will come as a surprise to many Catholics who associate the forgiveness of sins solely with the Sacrament of Penance. But upon reflection, we can easily see that if the Eucharist helps to increase our love for Christ, it must also keep us from the darkness of selfishness, which is sin. This is not to say that the Eucharist replaces our need for the Sacrament of Penance. It doesn't. Rather, it complements the work of sacramental reconciliation.

Communion renews, strengthens and deepens our incorporation into the Church, already achieved by Baptism (#1396)

During his last discourse, Jesus prayed to his Father: "May they all be one" (Jn 17:20), and he urged his disciples: "Love one another as I have loved you" (Jn 13:34). Through our participation in the Eucharist, we become bound ever more closely with the Church. As an ancient axiom goes: "The Church makes the Eucharist and the Eucharist makes the Church."

The Eucharist commits us to the poor (#1397)

The Catechism states: "To receive in truth the Body and Blood of Christ given up for us, we must recognize Christ in the poorest, his brethren." It then goes on to quote the challenging words from a homily of St. John Chrysostom, an Early Church Father:

> *You have tasted the Blood of the Lord, yet you do not recognize your brother . . . . You dishonor this table when you do not judge worthy of*

> *sharing your food someone judged worthy to take part in this meal... God freed you from all your sins and invited you here, but you have not become more merciful.*

In his first letter to the Corinthians, St. Paul reminds them that in sharing the Body of Christ in the Eucharist, they were also called to care for the poorest members of the community (1 Cor 11:17-34).

The Eucharist is our pledge of the glory to come (#1042-1405)
This fruit was most recognizable at the Last Supper when Jesus said: "I tell you I shall not drink again of this fruit of the vine until that day when I drink it anew in my Father's Kingdom" (Lk 22:18). Whenever we gather together to celebrate the Eucharist, we remember this promise of our Lord and turn our gaze towards him who is to come (#1403).

When we receive Holy Communion, we are publicly stating our willingness to stand with Jesus in his ongoing battle against all forms of evil and suffering in our world. The Calvary dimension of the Eucharist becomes real when we confront with love and courage the daily crosses and persecutions of life, such as difficult family and work situations, poor health, unjust structures of society that oppress and keep the poor in bondage. A central part of being sincere Eucharistic people is our willingness to feed the hungry, give drink to the thirsty, clothe the naked and visit the imprisoned (Mt 25:31-46).

Moments of Quiet
After the distribution of Holy Communion, the vessels are put aside and the presider is seated. Then follows *quiet meditation*

when we spend a few moments to contemplate on the meaning of Holy Communion and allow it to sink deep into our hearts. We may choose to either sit quietly in the presence of our Beloved or speak to him about the deepest concerns of our hearts. A medieval monk said: *"While we rest in him, he works in us."*

Sending forth Eucharistic ministers to the sick

At the beginning of this book, we quoted a description of the Eucharistic celebration in the early Church, which stated that the Eucharist was given to representatives of the community to be shared with the sick. In many parishes today, the presider, after Communion, sends forth lay ministers to take the Eucharist to the sick and homebound.

Prayer After Communion

The celebrant prays that the fruits of the mysteries which we have celebrated may take effect in our daily lives, especially the fruit of keeping our eyes on Jesus as we live and love in the world.

SUMMARY

- The Lord's Prayer, asking God to give us our daily bread and forgiving life's hurts, begins our immediate preparation for Holy Communion.
- Our participation in the Sign of Peace expresses our desire to be at peace with all people.
- Reception of Holy Communion with proper disposition of

heart deepens our union with Christ and his people, separates us from sin, commits us to sharing with the poor, and gives us the promise of everlasting life with Jesus.

QUESTIONS FOR PERSONAL AND GROUP REFLECTION

- Do you tend to see the reception of Holy Communion as a Jesus-and-me experience or as a Jesus-me-and-community experience—in other words, is your approach to the Eucharist individualistic or communal?
- The Catechism tells us that participation in the Eucharist commits us to the poor. To what extent are you aware of this aspect of the Eucharist?
- What can help you and others to avoid the danger of receiving the Eucharist in a rote and mindless way?

GOOD PRACTICE SUGGESTION

Develop the good practice of seeing the communal dimension of the Eucharist. Join in the singing of the Communion Song before and after you receive.

IV. CONCLUDING RITE

The Concluding Rite of the Mass consists of a blessing and sending forth into the world. As the presider raises his hand in blessing, the people sign themselves "in the name of the Father and of the Son and of the Holy Spirit," just as they did at the beginning of the Mass.

> *"To bless God means to praise God for his goodness and wonderful gifts. To bless a person is an action requesting that God continue to extend his generosity. In this final blessing the priest prays that the greatest of all benefits may be given in abundant measure to those who have shared in God's Word and Christ's Body. Such an action upon departure is found in the New Testament when Christ, before being taken up into heaven, 'raised his hands, and blessed the Apostles' (Lk 24:50)"* (The Mystery of Faith, p.121-122).

The presider then dismisses the assembly with these or similar words: "Go forth in peace to love and serve the Lord and each other." The dismissal is reminiscent of Christ's Great Commission to his Apostles: "Go forth into the whole world and teach all nations." Having received the gift of life, we are now sent forth to share that life with our brothers and sisters in the world. At the beginning of the Mass, we were enjoined to "Let us pray." Now we are instructed to "Let us act"—act as people touched by the Lord. We are sent forth to be the hands and feet of Jesus in the world. We are to be the bread of life for others. We are to share the Good News of God's love for all with others. We are sent forth to continue the saving work of Jesus in human history.

SUMMARY

- The Concluding Rite of the Mass consists of a blessing and commission.

QUESTION FOR PERSONAL AND GROUP REFLECTION

- How do you seek to live the Mass?

GOOD PRACTICE SUGGESTION

Develop the good practice of seeing yourself as being commissioned by Jesus and his Church to go forth and be an ambassador of Jesus in your family and workplace.

CONNECTING LITURGY AND LIFE

One cannot be truly engaged in the liturgy if they are not engaged in life. One supports the other. (Clara Dina Hinojosa)

It would seem that many people who attend Mass on Sunday see little connection between what happens in Church and what happens in their homes, neighborhoods, and workplaces. For many people, their "Thanks be to God" at the end of Mass may literally mean "Thank God, the Sunday obligation is taken care of; now let's get back to business as usual." Too few people are aware that the time spent in the world can be a means of personal sanctification just like the time spent in personal and communal prayer. Such separation of worship and life, of the sacred and the secular, is a perennial danger in Christian spirituality. It is too easy for us to lose sight of the beautiful fact that the Jesus who leads us in worship on Sunday morning is also at work in the kitchens and offices of life, seeking to build there "a kingdom of truth, justice, love and peace." (Preface, Feast of Christ the King).

At Mass, we celebrate the Paschal mystery of Jesus, i.e., his dying and rising, his passage back to the Father. But it is in our homes, neighborhoods, shopping centers, workplaces, etc., that we live the Paschal mystery. It is in these places that we literally enter (or fail to enter) into the death and Resurrection of Jesus. We enter into and share in the dying of Jesus when we are called to die to ourselves and our desires, when we experience rejection or misunderstanding, when we are gossiped about and treated unjustly, when we struggle with suffering, sickness, old age, evil and death. We enter into the dying of Jesus when we struggle with painful relationships at home, at work and at play. We enter into the victory and Resurrection of Jesus every time we make a decision to love, to give and receive forgiveness, to do what we can to change what can be changed and accept patiently what cannot be changed. We enter into and share in the victory and Resurrection of Jesus every time we let go of bitterness, jealousies, small-mindedness, and all the things that block us from communicating and experiencing the oneness of spirit that we pray for at Mass. All of the above examples and many others give us multiple opportunities to daily die and rise with Christ.

The authenticity and integrity of our weekly celebration of the Paschal mystery will be in direct relationship to our efforts to live the Paschal mystery in the hustle and bustle of daily life. If our daily lives reflect little of the dying and rising of Christ, then we can be sure that our Sunday celebration of those events, however devoutly attended or beautifully celebrated, will be of little interest to our Lord. In fact, he may well say of us, "These people honor me with their lips but their hearts are far from me" (Mk 7:6). Full, conscious and active participation does not just refer to liturgy but to all of life. Full, conscious and active participation refers to our relationships at home, work and at recreation. It is our response to God who is present and active in every aspect of our lives. Full, conscious and active participation means that we give ourselves totally to whatever we are doing at any particular moment.

When we come to Mass on Sunday, we bring with us to the altar of God our efforts, however fragile, to live the Paschal mystery.

During the Penitential Act, we give to the Lord our failures and we ask for his mercy and healing.

During the Liturgy of the Word, we look at our efforts to live the dying and rising of Christ and view them in the light of God's Word.

At the Presentation of the Gifts, we prepare the gifts of bread and wine, as well as our minds and hearts, to enter into Eucharistic Prayer and to receive the Body and Blood of Christ.

During the Eucharistic Prayer, we become mystically united in the perfect thanksgiving and self-offering of Jesus to his Father and our Father, praying that our efforts to give thanks and to surrender ourselves to him may be a little more generous.

During the Communion Rite, we receive food and drink from heaven, divine nourishment for life's journey. By our active participation in the Communion Rite, we give expression to the fact that we are members of the Body of Christ and want to be bread for our brothers and sisters as they journey through life.

Finally, at the Concluding Rite, we are once again sent forth into the marketplace to make a fresh effort to live the Paschal mystery of Jesus.

The time we spend in personal and communal prayer is a time to be recharged. This time is a call to be immersed in Christ so that we may re-enter even more intensely the arena of human activity. This time of union with Christ strengthens us as co-workers with the Lord who is molding us as he fashions "a new dwelling place and a new earth where justice will abide and whose blessedness will answer and surpass all the longings for peace which spring up in the human heart" (The Church in the Modern World #39). It is not a time of escape but a time of empowerment.

Much of what I have been saying about linking liturgy and life is beautifully summarized in these words of the late Cardinal Joseph Bernardin to the people of Chicago in his Pastoral Letter on the Liturgy. He writes:

> *The liturgy is not an extra something nice that may give us good feelings. It is our life, our very spirit. It is the source of our identity and renewal as a Church.*
>
> *When we let the liturgy shape us – from the ashes of Lent and the waters of baptism to the broken bread and poured out cup at every Sunday's Mass – then we shall find what it is "to put on Christ."*
>
> *Yet liturgy is also a humble reality, and participation in liturgy does not exhaust our duties as Christians. We shall be judged for attending to justice and giving witness to the truth, for hungry people fed and prisoners visited. Liturgy itself does not do these things. Yet good liturgy makes us a people whose hearts are set on such deeds. Liturgy is our communion, our strength, our nourishment, our song, our peace, our reminder, our promise. This singular meeting with the Lord Jesus leads*

us to make all the events and circumstances of our lives occasions for meeting Him. Liturgy is for me the bedrock of all my prayer and the measure of all my deeds.

SUMMARY

- In our celebration of the Eucharist, we memorialize the dying and rising of Christ. In our daily lives, we seek to live this core truth of our faith.
- The authenticity of our weekly celebration of the Paschal mystery will be in direct relationship to our efforts to live the Paschal mystery in our daily lives.

QUESTIONS FOR PERSONAL AND GROUP REFLECTION

- How do you seek to live the Paschal mystery in your daily life?
- Can you name a recent experience of dying to self that led to spiritual growth?

GOOD PRACTICE SUGGESTION

Seek to develop the good practice of connecting the dying and rising experiences of your daily life with your celebration of the Paschal mystery at Mass.

FOR OUR MEDITATION

COMMUNION

Comm-union!
The word rings out the Christian ideal.
A Church at one
a world at one
man one with man
man one with his God
man, through the Spirit,
one with the Father
one with the Son.

In the Mass
is this Communion
celebrated
signified
effected.

Therefore is the Mass
both summit and source
of all Christian activity.

For this, the Mass, was
the world created
the Church founded
the Word made flesh.

So that
at the heart of the Church
at the heart of the world
at the heart of the Divine Plan
is the MASS.

(Fr. Sean Swayne, Communion: The New Mass Rite)

FOR OUR MEDITATION

JESUS, JOY OF LOVING HEARTS

O Jesus, joy of loving hearts,
the fount of life and my true light,
we seek the peace your love imparts
and stand rejoicing in your sight.

We taste in you my living bread
and long to feast upon you still.
We drink of you my fountain head,
my thirsting soul to quench and fill.

For you my thirsting spirit yearns,
where'er our changing lot is cast;
glad when your presence we discern,
blest when our faith can hold you fast.

O Jesus, ever with us stay;
make all our moments calm and bright
O chase the night of sin away;
shed o'er the world your holy light.

(Quoted in U.S. Catholic Catechism for Adults, pp 229-230).

PART TWO: THE LITURGICAL YEAR

By means of the yearly cycle, the Church celebrates the holy mystery of Christ, from his Incarnation until Pentecost Day and the expectation of his coming again. (General Norms for the Liturgical Year Calendar, #17)

The Liturgical Year is the way Mother Church places before us the main events and teachings in the life of Jesus. When we remember those events and stories, we make them as real to us as they were to those who first experienced them. We bring past events into the now. So the Liturgical Year is not an historical look at past events, but the way that our Church invites us to enter and experience Christ who continues to be present and active in the events of our lives in the here and now.

SUNDAY

Sunday is the day of the Resurrection . . . . Sunday is the fundamental feast day . . . .
(Day of the Lord, #2)

Before seasons like Lent, Easter, Advent and Christmas evolved in our Church's liturgical calendar, there was Sunday. In the Church's year, Sunday is the primary and original feast day. It is still the heart of our Liturgical Year because it is the day that Christians celebrate Jesus' victory over sin and death. It is the day of the Resurrection of our Lord.

The term Sunday comes from the pre-Christian worship of the sun. From the sun, we receive light. In the Scriptures, Jesus is presented as the "true light that enlightens every person" (Jn 1:9).

The Lord's Day is the Church's official title for Sunday. It had a special meaning for the first Christians since it called to mind Christ's kingly victory over death. The title Lord also reminded the first generations of Christians that Jesus was Lord over all earthly lords, especially over the Roman Emperors who claimed divinity and persecuted Christians.

Sunday is also sometimes called the Eighth Day, a day which transcends time. In the Christian calendar, it is the first day of a new week or of a new creation. God created the world in six days, he rested on the seventh and he rose from the dead on the Eighth Day, the day a new creation started.

As Catholic Christians, we especially keep holy the Lord's Day by gathering together with our Church family to celebrate the Eucharist. Ideally, Sunday is also set aside by families as a day of relaxation and recreation. Of course, this is not always possible for people whose job demands that they work on Sunday. But, ideally, families should strive to prevent the temptations of the world to distract them from keeping holy the Lord's Day. As a pastor, I always find it inspiring to meet visiting families who make sure that Eucharistic participation is part of their Sunday.

SUMMARY

- Liturgical Year is used by the Church to place before us the main events and teachings in the life of Christ.
- Sunday is the primary and original feast day.

QUESTIONS FOR PERSONAL AND GROUP REFLECTION

- What does the term Liturgical Year mean to you?
- In an age when the secular world more and more ignores the sacredness of the Lord's Day, what can you or families do to keep the Lord's Day holy and special?

GOOD PRACTICE SUGGESTION

Develop the good practice of coming to Mass on Sunday and making it a day of rest and relaxation, not a day of work.

ADVENT/CHRISTMAS

Advent has a twofold character. It is a season (1) to prepare for Christmas when Christ's First Coming to us is remembered and (2) when that remembrance directs the mind and heart to await Christ's Second Coming at the end of time. Advent is thus a period for devout and joyful expectation. (General Norms for the Liturgical Year and Calendar, #39)

The word Advent means "coming." During the liturgical season we call Advent, we wait to celebrate the First Coming of Christ which occurred 2,000 years ago, and we wait for his Second Coming at some future time. We Christians live in an age between the two comings of Christ—in a period that scholars call the "already, but not yet." The Kingdom of God has already come into our midst in the Jesus event of 2,000 years ago, but Jesus has not yet come in his fullness. During the Advent season, we prepare to remember Christ's First Coming and, at the same time, we yearn for him to come again. It is like that period in a pregnancy when the child in the womb nears its delivery date and eagerly waits to be born.

Words most often associated with this season in our Church's calendar are longing, yearning, conversion, vigilance, joyful expectation and hope. Advent is a time of joy because Christ has already entered our world. It is also a time of expectation and hope for the Kingdom yet to come.

Living Advent

As followers of Christ who have to live in the world, we are most likely torn between two approaches to Christmas: the shopping mall expedition or the Advent preparation. While we cannot easily ignore all the hustle and bustle around us, we must do our best to live the Advent spirit during the weeks prior to Christmas.

Some suggestions:

- Have an Advent Wreath at home and light it several times during the season.
- Receive the Sacrament of Reconciliation as an excellent way to respond to John the Baptist's call to "prepare the way for the Lord."
- Include the poor in your Christmas budget. In our parish, we have an Angel Tree on which hangs hundreds of names of needy children. Parishioners are asked to bring gifts to the church office to be distributed to those needy children on the Saturday prior to Christmas, when they come with their families to our parish hall for their Christmas party.

- Use an Advent Daily Devotional to pray your way through this season. Most Catholic publishers come out with such devotionals each year.
- Connect all the beautiful Christmas lights to him who is the Light of our World.

Liturgical color: Violet

Christmas

The Word became flesh and made his dwelling among us, and we saw his glory, the glory as the Father's only Son, full of grace and truth.
(John 1:14)

Despite the secular overtones of the season, the word Christmas underscores for us its profound Christian and spiritual significance. The word Christmas is derived from the Old English Cristes Maesse, or Mass of Christ.

The liturgical season of Christmas begins on Christmas Eve and ends on the Sunday after the Epiphany, which is usually celebrated as the Baptism of the Lord. All the feasts within the octave of Christmas and beyond (e.g., St. Stephen, Holy Innocents, Holy Family, Mary the Mother of God, Epiphany) are components of this one great event – the Divine in our midst, God manifesting his divine presence in a human way to the Jewish and Gentile world. All of the feasts within the season of Christmas are "like polished facets or a precious gemstone, each giving us a different view of the mystery we celebrate" (Entering into the Spirit of Christmas, by Fr. Lawrence Mick, Today's Parish, Vol.37, No.3, p.37). The heart of this season is summarized in the name Emmanuel – God in our midst. As Christians, we believe that in good times and in bad, our God is not some distant deity, but one who is with us during every twist and turn of life's journey.

Living Christmas

In the thirteenth century, Meister Eckhart, mystic and theologian, wrote: "Christmas is the celebration of the birth of Jesus, as God-made-man *in time*, but if his birth is not *reproduced* in my soul, what advantage is this celebration to me?" Another mystic from the sixteenth century, Angela Sitesio, wrote: "Even if Christ were to be born a thousand times in Bethlehem, but is not born in my soul, I am lost forever." It is obvious from the words of these two lovers of God that besides the physical birth of Christ in Bethlehem, there is also the spiritual birth of Jesus which needs to take place in every soul. This is sometimes called Christmas of the Soul, as opposed to the external aspects of the season, e.g., decorations, card-writing, parties, shopping, gift-giving, etc., all of which have a place in Christmas. Christmas of the Soul involves opening our hearts to Jesus and seeking to live as he lived. This is what we must especially focus on and seek to live.

Liturgical colors: White and Gold

SUMMARY

- Advent is a preparation focusing on two great events: the First and the Second Coming of Christ.
- Christmas celebrates the Word made flesh, God in our midst, as one of us.

QUESTIONS FOR PERSONAL AND GROUP REFLECTION

- What do you and your family do to make Jesus the main focus of the Advent Season?
- What can you do to live Christmas of the Soul?

GOOD PRACTICE SUGGESTION

Develop the *good practice* of having an Advent Wreath in your home and lighting its candles several times each week to remind you of the true spirit of the Advent/Christmas Season.

LENT

Lent is a preparation for the celebration of Easter. The Lenten liturgy disposes both catechumens and the faithful to celebrate the paschal mystery: catechumens, through the several stages of Christian initiation; the faithful, through reminders of their own baptism and through penitential practices. (General Norms for the Liturgical Year and the Calendar, #27)

The season of Lent begins on Ash Wednesday and ends prior to the Lord's Supper on Holy Thursday. Lent comes from the Anglo-Saxon word lencten for springtime. In Christian spirituality, the season of Lent is intended to be a spiritual springtime for the unbaptized (called elect) and also for the baptized. On Ash Wednesday, when our Lenten journey begins, the prophet Joel says to us: "Rend your hearts, not your garments." Commenting on these words from the first reading, Thomas Merton writes:

"Rendering only your garments lets in nothing but air, rendering our hearts lets out sin and lets in the clean air of God's spring."

Baptismal focus

In the early centuries of the Church when the catechumenate developed, Lent was the final period of preparation for the unbaptized who were discerned to be ready for full initiation into the Church on Easter Vigil. For the already baptized, Lent was an opportunity to deepen their baptismal commit-ment to Christ. The baptismal focus has been restored in our own time.

Living Lent

If we embrace the baptismal focus of Lent, it will most likely change the way we approach the season. The emphasis will not be primarily on giving up something but rather our doing whatever will deepen our baptismal commitment to Christ.

Lent rooted in Baptism will mean taking a serious look at where there is sin in our lives, where there is need for repentance and conversion, where there is need to weed out, with God's help, sinful attitudes and behaviors that hinder us from being more effective witnesses to Christ and his message.

Practicing the three traditional spiritual exercises of prayer, fasting and almsgiving (Mt 6:1-13) can be a big help as we seek to prepare for Baptism or for renewal of our baptismal commitment to Christ. Properly approached and utilized, prayer, fasting and almsgiving will facilitate a change of heart and behavior in our lives.

In and through authentic prayer, we create a space for God in our lives and allow him to have his way with us. In prayer, we open ourselves to God asking him to show us where there is sin in our lives and where there is need for conversion and healing. Through fasting from certain foods and drinks, we allow ourselves to experience in a small way the extreme hunger that millions of people in our world experience daily. We can also fast from excessive use of television, radio and internet, and from sins of the tongue. In the spiritual life, fasting is never an end in itself. It is intended to facilitate a closer walk with Christ and a greater solidarity with the poor. Through almsgiving, we also express oneness with our less fortunate brothers and sisters all over the world. In many parishes, Operation Rice Bowl, a ministry of Catholic Relief Services, is a way to connect with the poor of the world.

Two final suggestions for living the Spirit of Lent: First, receive the Sacrament of Reconciliation. Fruitful reception of this sacrament will certainly ready our hearts on Easter Vigil to say a stronger No! to Satan and sin, and a stronger Yes! to Jesus and all that he stands for. Second, take time to pray the Stations of the Cross, making a special effort to experience the immense sufferings of our beloved Savior as he poured out his life for us that we might experience the abundance of God's love and salvation.

Liturgical color: Purple

SUMMARY

- For the Elect (candidates for Baptism), Lent is a time of spiritual preparation for the reception of the sacraments of initiation. For the already baptized, Lent is a time of spiritual preparation for the renewal of their baptismal commitment.

QUESTIONS FOR PERSONAL AND GROUP REFLECTION

- In recent years, the Church has restored the baptismal character of Lent. How does such a focus impact the way you approach Lent?
- What spiritual exercises will help you to deepen your baptismal commitment to the Lord?

GOOD PRACTICE SUGGESTION

Develop the *good practice* of praying for and supporting all who are preparing to receive the sacraments of initiation in your parish.

EASTER TRIDUUM

The Easter Triduum of the Passion and Resurrection of Christ is the culmination of the entire liturgical year. (General Norms, #18)

While in popular culture the season of Christmas receives the most attention, the truth is that the Easter Triduum is the culmination or high point of the entire Liturgical Year. The Triduum begins with the celebration of the Lord's Supper on Holy Thursday and concludes with Evening Prayer on Easter Sunday evening.

The term Triduum is from the Latin tres dies (three days). But is the Triduum three or four days – Thursday, Friday, Saturday and Sunday? In liturgical time, the Church follows the ancient Jewish practice of reckoning a day by starting from the evening before. So the first day of the Triduum is Thursday evening to Friday evening, the second day is Friday evening to Saturday evening, and the third day is Saturday evening to Sunday evening.

Our Church tells us that the Triduum is not so much three distinct rites (the Lord's Supper, Good Friday and the Easter Vigil) as one continuous celebration with three parts. The unified nature of the three-in-one liturgies is underlined by the omission of a concluding rite on Holy Thursday and Good Friday. These two liturgies are left hanging, so to speak—incomplete without that which follows. It is as if the omission of a concluding rite on Holy Thursday and Good Friday is saying to us: We are not done yet... to be continued. In the same manner, Good Friday and Easter Vigil do not have the normal introductory rites. On Good Friday, the presider processes in silence and prostrates himself before the sanctuary. Easter Vigil begins outdoors with the assembly gathered around the Easter Fire. Though the Triduum is the most sacred and most important three days in our Church's liturgical calendar, they are not holy days of obligation. To declare them holy days would be stating the obvious, like making it obligatory for us to celebrate Independence Day.

Meaning

Just as we do not pretend that Christ is born again at Christmas, so also we do not make believe that he dies and rises again during the Triduum. We were not there when Christ hung on the Cross and rose from the dead. Yet, in another sense, we were there. Fr. Lawrence Mick explains our presence in this way:

> *Yet by the time Easter Sunday arrives, we can say: Yes, we are there when he dies and rises constantly in the lives of his followers. Yes, we are there when we witness the victory over sin and death as it is revealed in the elect who enter the watery grave and rise to new life. Yes, we are there when we all enter again into the Death and Resurrection of the Lord,*

so that we, too, die more completely to sin and rise renewed to live in newness of life. (The Spirit of the Triduum, *Today's Parish*, Vol.37, No.6, p.20)

This dying and rising is the foundation of our life of faith. Enacted in its fullest expression at the Easter Vigil each year, the paschal mystery calls us all back to the source and invites us to renew and deepen our commitment. As the Triduum is the core of the liturgical year, so the Vigil is the core of the Triduum, the point to which all climbs and from which all flows. (ibid, p.18)

Now, for a brief look at each of the three celebrations of the Triduum.

Thursday: Mass of the Lord's Supper

The opening movement of the Triduum is the Mass of the Lord's Supper. While this celebration recalls the institution of the Eucharist and the priesthood, its prime focus is the dying and rising of Christ, as summed up nicely in the entrance antiphon: "We should glory in the cross of our Lord Jesus Christ for he is our salvation, our life and our resurrection; through him we are saved and made free."

A very important ritual in this celebration is the *Washing of the Feet*. This beautiful act reminds us that leadership in God's kingdom is a call to humble service (see also Mt 20:24-28) and that living the Eucharist involves a readiness to lay down our lives for one another.

Good Friday: Celebration of the Lord's Passion

We may wonder why our Church calls this day *Good* Friday rather than *Bad* Friday. It is called *Good* Friday because this is the day Jesus took on the powers of evil and triumphed over them. On Good Friday, we listen to John's account of the Passion. In contrast to the accounts of Matthew, Mark and Luke, John presents Jesus as a kingly figure very much in control of events. It was on Good Friday when Jesus freely laid down his life so that we may have a share in God's abundant life. Good Friday is a day of sober joy.

The celebration has three parts: Liturgy of the Word, Veneration of the Cross, and Communion Service. Hosts consecrated on Holy Thursday are ministered on Good Friday.

The Easter Vigil

St. Augustine called this celebration the *Mother of all Vigils*. It is the holiest night of the Church year when:

- we celebrate Christ's victory over sin, death and evil.
- Christians are made.
- we, the baptized, renew our baptismal commitment to Christ.

In the Early Church, this liturgy went from sunset to sunrise. So our two- or three-hour liturgies are, in a way, mini-vigils. The Easter Vigil celebration has four parts:

- ***Service of Light.*** All gather outside of Church with the Elect around the Easter fire which is blessed and lit. The new Easter or Paschal Candle is blessed and lit from the fire. All process into the dark Church with candles lit from the Paschal candle. Then the beautiful Exultet is sung which proclaims the meaning and wonder of this most Holy Night: "This is the night when Jesus Christ broke the chains of death and rose triumphant from the grave."
- ***Liturgy of the Word.*** On this night, we listen to several readings from the Old and New Testament which proclaim our salvation and history and speak of creation, liberation, new life and Resurrection. Hopefully, we all realize that the God who was present and active in the lives of ancient Israel and in the life of Jesus, is also present in our midst on this holy night, calling us to live as redeemed and freed children of a loving God.
- ***Liturgy of Baptism.*** This is the night our Elect have been looking forward to for months or years. Regarding this part of the Vigil, Fr. Mick writes: "At the font we see the death and resurrection of Christ played out before our eyes. Here we remember who we are, people who have died and risen in Christ, people who have been anointed by the Holy Spirit, disciples who share at the table of the Lord to be strengthened to carry on the mission of Christ in our time. That's why we all renew our baptismal promises after the newly baptized emerge from the font" (ibid. p.21).
- ***Liturgy of the Eucharist.*** Having died and risen with Christ in the waters of Baptism and having been anointed with chrism for mission, the neophytes and all present come to

the Table of the Lord to be fed with the Body and Blood of Christ, their nourishment for the journey.

Easter Sunday Masses are an extension of the Easter Vigil, during which all present renew their baptismal commitment to Christ. The Evening Prayer on Easter Sunday concludes the Triduum.

THE FIFTY DAYS OF EASTER

The fifty days from Easter Sunday to Pentecost are celebrated in joyful exultation as one feast day, better as one great Sunday. (General Norms, #22)

For Christians, the term Easter means Christ is the sun that rises at dawn—in the east. The Council of Nicaea in 315 decreed that Easter Day should be celebrated on the Sunday following the first new moon after the spring equinox.

In the Church's liturgical calendar, Easter is not just a day but a season that spans fifty days—from Easter day until Pentecost. For our ancestors in the faith, fifty days was a symbol of eternity. It takes seven weeks to tell the whole story.

During the Fifty Days of Easter, our Church invites us to immerse ourselves in the Paschal mystery—in the victory of Christ over sin and death. Reflecting on the Easter season, Fr. Mick writes: "Easter is the harvest from seeds planted during

Lent that blossomed in the Triduum. It is a time to bask in the afterglow of the Easter fire and candle, to enjoy the freshness of being cleansed and reborn, to dwell in the power of the Spirit of God and to savor the Body and Blood of the Lord given to us as food and drink to sustain our new life" (Entering into the Spirit of Easter, Today's Parish, Vol.37, No.7, p.19).

Looking at the Easter season through the lens of the RCIA (Rite of Christian Initiation of Adults) process, Easter is a period of mystagogy not only for the newly baptized but also for the entire Christian community (RCIA #244). *Mystagogy* is a Greek word for *savoring the mysteries*. It is a time for the Christian community to savor ever more deeply its understanding and appreciation of the mysteries of the Christian faith. It is a time to ponder ever more fully what God has done for us in Christ. During the Easter season, we also ponder the beginnings of our Church, the meaning of discipleship, the gift of the Holy Spirit, and the mission entrusted upon all the baptized.

Living the Easter Season

Living joyfully the Fifty Days of Easter is strangely much more challenging than living the penitential Forty Days of Lent. Because of our formation, we are usually up for the challenge of Lent. We have been raised to see Lent as a time for *extra effort*. In contrast, we have little or no formation that prepares us to celebrate the Fifty Days of Easter. Also, oddly enough, most of us seem to do better at entering into Lenten penitential practices than into Easter feasting. In addition, the Easter season in most parishes includes the celebration of Mother's Day, First Communion, Confirmation and graduations. It is not easy to stay focused on the true meaning of Easter while all these other celebrations are also occurring.

Some suggestions:

- Obtain a daily devotional for the Fifty Days of Easter to help you to pray with our Church and stay focused on the real meaning of this season.
- Use this season to deepen your understanding and appreciation of the sacraments of initiation: Baptism, Confirmation and Eucharist.
- Take time to meet, greet and welcome those who were initiated into our Church during the Easter Vigil.
- Reflect on how you are seeking to live the Paschal mystery in your daily life—the dying and rising of Christ. Easter is not just about what happened 2,000 years ago. It is also about what is happening to us now, how the pattern of Jesus' dying and rising occurs in the ups and downs of our daily lives.

Liturgical color: White or Gold; Red on Pentecost Sunday

SUMMARY

- The Easter Triduum is the high point or culmination of the whole Liturgical Year.
- The Easter Season is a fifty-day celebration of Christ's victory over sin and death, and our opportunity to immerse ourselves in the Paschal mystery.

QUESTIONS FOR PERSONAL AND GROUP REFLECTION

- "Dying he destroyed our death. Rising he restored our life." What do these words mean in your life?
- Who are the people in your community who model servant leadership?
- How willing are you to seek out those who were received into your Church family during the Easter Vigil and extend hospitality to them?

GOOD PRACTICE SUGGESTION

Develop the *good practice* of joining your Church family's celebration of the Easter Triduum.

ORDINARY TIME

Apart from those seasons having their own distinctive character, thirty-three or thirty-four weeks remain in the yearly cycle that do not celebrate a specific aspect of the mystery of Christ. Rather, especially on the Sundays, they are devoted to the mystery of Christ in all its aspect. This period is known as Ordinary Time. (General Norms, #43)

The term Ordinary Time refers to the 34 Sundays of the Liturgical Year that are not part of the Advent/Christmas and Lent/Triduum/Easter seasons. Wrapped around these two major seasons are 34 Sundays.

There are two periods of Ordinary Time in our Liturgical Year.

- The first period begins on the day after the Baptism of the Lord and continues until Shrove Tuesday, the day before Ash Wednesday.

- The second period begins on the Monday after Pentecost Sunday and continues until the Saturday before the first Sunday of Advent. The first two Sundays of Ordinary Time in this period are always replaced by two Solemnities: The Solemnity of the Most Holy Trinity and the Solemnity of the Body and Blood of Christ. The last Sunday of Ordinary Time in this period is always replaced by the Solemnity of Christ the King.

The term Ordinary Time refers to ordinal or counted time: first, second, third, etc. The term is not intended to mean unimportant. Every day and every Sunday in our Liturgical Year are important because every day is a day that the Lord has made and every Sunday is a celebration of the Lord's Resurrection. Yet in another sense, Ordinary Time is ordinary in that it does not focus primarily on the major events in Christ's life that we celebrate during the two major seasons of our Church year. We might say that Ordinary Time developed not so much for what it is, but for what it is not – it is not Advent, Christmas, Lent or Easter Time. In his excellent little book, The Liturgical Year, Dan Connors writes:

> *We should have a special feeling for Ordinary Time, because most of our lives are spent doing very ordinary things: working, eating, paying bills, worrying, shopping, and driving. These are not very exciting, but they make up the rhythms of our lives much more than do birthdays and special occasions. We are called to listen to God's voice, not just during the special seasons of the year, but always. We are to carry out our Christian mission, not just on the holy days, but always. We are to help*

the poor and work for justice, not just at Thanksgiving and Christmas, but always. Ordinary Time is an opportunity to be the Body of Christ in the midst of everyday life. It is an opportunity to experience how God calls us to holiness in our daily rhythm of waking and resting, working and playing, laughing and worrying. When we can find God here, how much more glorious the great seasons of our year will be! (p.42)

Living Ordinary Time

The above quote by Dan Connors points us in the right direction when it comes to living this time of our Liturgical Year. This is a time for us to seek and respond to God as he comes to us in the ordinary events and encounters of daily life. Seeking, finding and responding to God in the happenings of daily life are the main goal of the spiritual life.

Praying the Scriptures that are read in Church every day is another excellent way to live Ordinary Time. An excellent aid to a fruitful meditation on the daily Scriptures can be found in The Word Among Us. This monthly devotional contains the text of every daily and Sunday Scripture readings of our Church Year. It also has a reflection on one of the readings. In addition, it has several other articles on various aspects of the spiritual life and articles on some of the saints.

Liturgical color: Green, the symbol of hope

SUMMARY

- Ordinary Time refers to the 34 Sundays of our Liturgical Year that are wrapped around the two major seasons of our Church year.
- Ordinary Time is our opportunity to become holy as we go about our daily lives.

QUESTIONS FOR PERSONAL AND GROUP REFLECTION

- What has helped you to become more attentive and responsive to the presence of the Holy Spirit in your daily life?
- What can help you to do ordinary things with extraordinary love?

GOOD PRACTICE SUGGESTION

Develop the *good practice* of seeking God's presence in the nitty-gritty details of daily life.

SANCTORAL CYCLE: SOLEMNITIES, FEASTS, AND MEMORIALS

As it celebrates the mystery of Christ in the yearly cycle, the church also venerates with a particular love Mary, the Mother of God, and sets before the devotion of the faithful the memory of the martyrs and other saints. (General Norms, #8)

Our Liturgical Year is divided into two main parts which occur simultaneously on two other schedules: *Temporal Cycle* and *Sanctoral Cycle*.

This is where our Liturgical Year becomes a bit complex. It is not always clear what belongs in the Temporal cycle and what belongs in the Sanctoral Cycle. Keep in mind that the following breakdown does have some exceptions.

- *Temporal Cycle* includes all the Sundays of the year and some Solemnities, e.g., Ascension of the Lord, and some Feasts when they fall on a Sunday, e.g., Birth of John the Baptist.
- *Sanctoral Cycle* refers mainly to feasts of saints. These so-called feasts have their own hierarchy or levels: Solemnities, (Assumption of Mary, All Saints Day), Feasts (Birth of Mary, Conversion of St. Paul), and Memorials (St. Francis of Assisi, St. Thomas Aquinas).

Living the Sanctoral Cycle

Gratefully, our concern does not need to be what belongs in the above two cycles. We leave that task to our official liturgical leaders. For us, living the Sanctoral Cycle primarily involves becoming *informed and inspired* by the lives of the wonderful men and women who have become outstanding examples of Christian life. As Catholic Christians, we can be most grateful for this part of our spirituality and liturgical life. Men and women who lived in times and places, and very different from our own, continue to give us wisdom and inspiration when it comes to our own efforts to follow Christ.

If you wish to become more informed about the Saints and the Blesseds (candidates for canonization) who make up the Sanctoral Cycle, I recommend the book *Saint of the Day—Updated and Expanded,* the 2013 edition, St. Anthony Messenger Press. The book is a whole calendar year of saints' feastdays with a short biography of each saint, a comment linking the example of the saint's life to our own, and often a quote from one of the saint's writings.

SUMMARY

- In and through the *Sanctoral Cycle*, the Church places before us men and women whose lives continue to give us wisdom and inspiration as we struggle to follow Jesus and his Gospel values.

QUESTION FOR PERSONAL AND GROUP REFLECTION

- Who is your favorite saint? Why?

GOOD PRACTICE SUGGESTION

Develop the *good practice* of becoming more informed about the lives of holy men and women who can inspire you in your endeavor to live a good and holy life.

RESOURCES

The General Instruction of the Roman Missal, Third Edition 2008, Washington, D.C.: USCC, 2003.

General Norms for the Liturgical Year, The Catholic Liturgical Library, 1998-2010.

Introduction to the Order of the Mass, Washington, D.C.: USCC, 2003.

Catechism of the Catholic Church, 2nd ed., Washington D.C.: USCC.

Carter, Joan. The Mass, its Rituals, Roots and Relevance in our Lives.

Sri, Edward. A Biblical Walk Through the Mass.

Johnson, Lawrence. The Mystery of Faith, (Third Edition 2011)

Mick, Rev. Lawrence. Articles in Today's Parish, Vols. 3,6,7.

Connors, Dan. The Liturgical Year, Mystic, CT: Twenty-Third Publications.